"This series is a tremendous resource for thos
understanding of how the gospel is woven tl
pastors and scholars doing gospel business fro.. ... ...
logical feast preparing God's people to apply the entire Bible to all of life with heart and mind
wholly committed to Christ's priorities."

BRYAN CHAPELL, President Emeritus, Covenant Theological Seminary; Senior Pastor,
Grace Presbyterian Church, Peoria, Illinois

"Mark Twain may have smiled when he wrote to a friend, 'I didn't have time to write you a
short letter, so I wrote you a long letter.' But the truth of Twain's remark remains serious and
universal, because well-reasoned, compact writing requires extra time and extra hard work.
And this is what we have in the Crossway Bible study series *Knowing the Bible*. The skilled
authors and notable editors provide the contours of each book of the Bible as well as the
grand theological themes that bind them together as one Book. Here, in a 12-week format,
are carefully wrought studies that will ignite the mind and the heart."

R. KENT HUGHES, Visiting Professor of Practical Theology, Westminster Theological
Seminary

"*Knowing the Bible* brings together a gifted team of Bible teachers to produce a high-quality
series of study guides. The coordinated focus of these materials is unique: biblical content,
provocative questions, systematic theology, practical application, and the gospel story of
God's grace presented all the way through Scripture."

PHILIP G. RYKEN, President, Wheaton College

"These *Knowing the Bible* volumes provide a significant and very welcome variation on the
general run of inductive Bible studies. This series provides substantial instruction, as well as
teaching through the very questions that are asked. *Knowing the Bible* then goes even further
by showing how any given text links with the gospel, the whole Bible, and the formation of
theology. I heartily endorse this orientation of individual books to the whole Bible and the
gospel, and I applaud the demonstration that sound theology was not something invented
later by Christians, but is right there in the pages of Scripture."

GRAEME L. GOLDSWORTHY, former lecturer, Moore Theological College; author,
According to Plan, Gospel and Kingdom, The Gospel in Revelation, and *Gospel and Wisdom*

"What a gift to earnest, Bible-loving, Bible-searching believers! The organization and
structure of the Bible study format presented through the *Knowing the Bible* series is so well
conceived. Students of the Word are led to understand the content of passages through per-
ceptive, guided questions, and they are given rich insights and application all along the way
in the brief but illuminating sections that conclude each study. What potential growth in
depth and breadth of understanding these studies offer! One can only pray that vast numbers
of believers will discover more of God and the beauty of his Word through these rich studies."

BRUCE A. WARE, Professor of Christian Theology, The Southern Baptist Theological
Seminary

KNOWING THE BIBLE

J. I. Packer, Theological Editor
Dane C. Ortlund, Series Editor
Lane T. Dennis, Executive Editor

•   •   •   •   •   •

Genesis
Exodus
Leviticus
Numbers
Deuteronomy
Joshua
Judges
Ruth and Esther
1–2 Samuel
1–2 Kings
1–2 Chronicles
Ezra and Nehemiah
Job

Psalms
Proverbs
Ecclesiastes
Song of Solomon
Isaiah
Jeremiah
Lamentations,
Habakkuk, and
Zephaniah
Ezekiel
Daniel
Hosea
Joel, Amos, and
Obadiah

Jonah, Micah, and
Nahum
Haggai, Zechariah,
and Malachi
Matthew
Mark
Luke
John
Acts
Romans
1 Corinthians
2 Corinthians
Galatians

Ephesians
Philippians
Colossians and
Philemon
1–2 Thessalonians
1–2 Timothy and
Titus
Hebrews
James
1–2 Peter and Jude
1–3 John
Revelation

•   •   •   •   •   •

J. I. PACKER is the former Board of Governors' Professor of Theology at Regent College (Vancouver, BC). Dr. Packer earned his DPhil at the University of Oxford. He is known and loved worldwide as the author of the best-selling book *Knowing God*, as well as many other titles on theology and the Christian life. He serves as the General Editor of the ESV Bible and as the Theological Editor for the *ESV Study Bible*.

LANE T. DENNIS is CEO of Crossway, a not-for-profit publishing ministry. Dr. Dennis earned his PhD from Northwestern University. He is Chair of the ESV Bible Translation Oversight Committee and Executive Editor of the *ESV Study Bible*.

DANE C. ORTLUND is Chief Publishing Officer at Crossway. He is a graduate of Covenant Theological Seminary (MDiv, ThM) and Wheaton College (BA, PhD). Dr. Ortlund has authored several books and scholarly articles in the areas of Bible, theology, and Christian living.

JOSHUA
A 12-WEEK STUDY

Trent Hunter

WHEATON, ILLINOIS

Crossway is a publishing ministry of Good News Publishers.

VP		29	28	27	26	25	24	23	22	21	20	19
15	14	13	12	11	10	9	8	7	6	5	4	3

TABLE OF CONTENTS

Series Preface: J. I. Packer and Lane T. Dennis. 6

Week 1:   Overview. 7

Week 2:   An Old Promise, a New Leader (1:1–18) 13

Week 3:   Sending in the Spies, Finding a Surprise (2:1–24). 21

Week 4:   Crossing the Jordan, Getting Right with God (3:1–5:15). 29

Week 5:   A Foolish Plan, a Decisive Outcome (6:1–27). 37

Week 6:   Two Piles of Stones, One Crucial Lesson (7:1–8:35) 45

Week 7:   Taking More Land, Hanging More Kings (9:1–12:24). 53

Week 8:   Putting Down Roots, Receiving God's Inheritance (13:1–19:51). . . 61

Week 9:   Cities for Justice, People for Worship (20:1–21:45). 69

Week 10: An Altar of Remembrance, an Unforgettable Altercation
            (22:1–34). 75

Week 11: Joshua Dies in the Land, the Promise of Rest Lives On
            (23:1–24:33) 83

Week 12: Summary and Conclusion 91

SERIES PREFACE

KNOWING THE BIBLE, as the series title indicates, was created to help readers know and understand the meaning, the message, and the God of the Bible. Each volume in the series consists of 12 units that progressively take the reader through a clear, concise study of that book of the Bible. In this way, any given volume can fruitfully be used in a 12-week format either in group study, such as in a church-based context, or in individual study. Of course, these 12 studies could be completed in fewer or more than 12 weeks, as convenient, depending on the context in which they are used.

Each study unit gives an overview of the text at hand before digging into it with a series of questions for reflection or discussion. The unit then concludes by highlighting the gospel of grace in each passage ("Gospel Glimpses"), identifying whole-Bible themes that occur in the passage ("Whole-Bible Connections"), and pinpointing Christian doctrines that are affirmed in the passage ("Theological Soundings").

The final component to each unit is a section for reflecting on personal and practical implications from the passage at hand. The layout provides space for recording responses to the questions proposed, and we think readers need to do this to get the full benefit of the exercise. The series also includes definitions of key words. These definitions are indicated by a note number in the text and are found at the end of each chapter.

Lastly, for help in understanding the Bible in this deeper way, we would urge the reader to use the ESV Bible and the *ESV Study Bible*, which are available online at esv.org. The *Knowing the Bible* series is also available online.

May the Lord greatly bless your study as you seek to know him through knowing his Word.

J. I. Packer
Lane T. Dennis

WEEK 1: OVERVIEW

▲

An obscure, landless people invade a land with fortified cities, trained armies, and powerful kings? This is exactly what Israel did—with great success!—under Joshua's leadership. Joshua is a fascinating narrative, but it is not easy to read, and its significance for the Christian can be difficult to grasp. There are familiar lines in this book, including God's famous command to Joshua ("Be strong and courageous"; 1:9) and Joshua's covenantal vow ("As for me and my house, we will serve the LORD"; 24:15). While these verses have meaning for Christians today, as we will see later their immediate context is very different from our own: Joshua is the leader of a nation commanded by God to invade the ancient land of Canaan and kill all of its inhabitants. It can be difficult to understand why this kind of story is in the Bible—for the questions it raises and for the obscurity of its ancient history.

For many, the Bible presents enigmatic challenges, especially in the narrative portions of the Old Testament, like Joshua. Nevertheless, according to God's wisdom, this book *is* in the Bible and is profitable for teaching, reproof, correction, and training in righteousness (see 2 Tim. 3:16). As we will see, Joshua is as marvelous as it is at first mysterious. Joshua will teach us about the unfailing promises of God springing from his unfailing faithfulness. It will teach us about the justice of God against sin and the great mercy of God toward sinners.

In fact, you might be surprised to learn that this is a book about heaven and hell, sin and salvation; it is about Jesus—and it is about you, the twenty-first-century reader. What Israel ultimately needs is something much greater than a plot of land on which to live. Joshua and the people will settle the land, but they will also die there because of sin's curse. What they need is a cross and a new creation. And while the story of Joshua doesn't get us all the way there, it makes us long for that eschatological[1] reality. It makes us long with great expectation for this cross and for a city whose maker and builder is God, for a heavenly city, for a new creation in which everything is right and everything is at rest.

It will take some work to follow the Bible's lead in making these connections, but we will make them before we're done, and the journey will be worth it. As we read and study together, may we rejoice in a fuller vision of the kind of Savior Christ is, the kind of people Christ saves, and the kind of salvation Christ brings.

Placing It in the Larger Story

Central to the book of Joshua is God's promise of land. The very structure of the story makes this clear, as seen in the outline provided below. Though often in a more subtle fashion, this theme stretches from the first page of the Bible to the last. The promise of the land of Canaan has its origin in God's promise to Abraham (Gen. 12:1–3). God called Abraham from among the nations and gave him several promises, including land, a nation, and blessing to the rest of the nations through him. The story of Joshua develops each of these promises, but its focus and emphasis is clearly on God's promise of land.

Frequently in Joshua we'll see references to the promises given to Abraham and his offspring. And yet God's promise of land has a certain broader context. The land theme goes further back than Abraham. God made Adam in his image and placed him in Eden. Adam and his race were to multiply and fill the earth, exercising dominion over it. But that didn't happen. Instead, Adam turned from trusting God. As promised, God cursed Adam with death and sent the first human pair outside the garden. This is where the story of land begins. The entire salvation story of the Bible is a response to what happened in Eden. When God promised Abraham a place of blessing, he essentially promised him what was lost in the fall—a place for the enjoyment of God's presence, a return to Eden. This is why the land of promise is regularly referred to as "like the garden of Eden" (Gen. 13:10; Isa. 51:3; Ezek. 36:35; Joel 2:3).

Orbiting around the theme of land in Joshua are numerous other themes crucial to the Bible's salvation story:

- In the land, God's people will experience *rest*.
- The land is a gift from God *promised* to his people.
- God's *covenants*[2] with Abraham and Moses provide the context for the story of Israel inheriting the land.
- *Obedience* is required for entrance into the blessing of the land, even as *disobedience* will lead to cursing and failure to take the land.
- The Lord *judges* the Canaanite inhabitants in the land by means of his people.
- The Lord fights for his people as the *Divine Warrior* to judge and drive out the inhabitants of the land.
- The land is never fully obtained, evidencing a *tension in the storyline* leading us to Christ by showing our need for a new covenant with a fully obedient covenant mediator.

The book of Joshua is a story of salvation within the Bible's larger story of salvation through Christ, and each of these themes has a part to play in pulling the story along. Indeed, Jesus will come as a new Joshua to "save his people from their sins" (Matt. 1:21). Through the story of Joshua, God is advancing his promise to bless his people with rest in the land. He will do this through his man Joshua, as Joshua and the people entrust themselves to the Lord with full obedience to his Word.

Key Verse

"The LORD gave to Israel all the land that he swore to give to their fathers. And they took possession of it, and they settled there." (Josh. 21:43)

Date and Historical Background

The historical setting for the book of Joshua is given in the first line of the book: "After the death of Moses" (1:1). This time marker indicates the situation of God's people. Forty years had passed since the exodus, years spent wandering and waiting to cross the Jordan and inherit the land promised by God. Like a sequel to a movie, this book opens on the cusp of the rest of the story. As the first book written after the death of Moses, Joshua picks up and develops many of the themes established in the first five books of the Bible.

The author of Joshua is not specified. And while some have suggested Joshua as the author, the recurring phrase "to this day" (4:9; 5:9; 6:25; etc.) seems to indicate that the book was written later, or at least that an editor updated the book at a later date.

Outline

I. Crossing into the Land (1:1–5:15)

    A. Joshua receives and gives his marching orders (1:1–18)

    B. Joshua sends in the spies and receives good news (2:1–24)

    C. Israel crosses the Jordan and God does wonders (3:1–4:24)

    D. Israel renews the covenant and Joshua meets the Lord's commander (5:1–15)

II. Taking the Land (6:1–12:24)

    A. Joshua takes Jericho, a paradigm for victory (6:1–27)

    B. Achan sins and Israel falls at Ai, a paradigm for defeat (7:1–26)

    C. Israel deals with Achan and takes Ai (8:1–35)

    D. Israel covenants with some Gibeonites and thus Gentiles get in on salvation (9:1–27)

    E. Joshua defends Gibeon and takes the south (10:1–43)

    F. Joshua takes the north and the author takes an inventory of kings (11:1–12:24)

III. Dividing the Land (13:1–21:45)

    A. Allotments for the eastern territories (13:1–33)

    B. Allotments for the western territories (14:1–19:51)

    C. Provision for justice and worship (20:1–21:45)

IV. Serving the Lord in the Land (22:1–24:33)

    A. Joshua's parting speech to the eastern tribes (22:1–34)

    B. Joshua's parting speech to Israel's leaders (23:1–16)

    C. Joshua's parting speech to the nation (24:1–33)

As You Get Started

One way to get a sense of Joshua's message is to grasp its context. Read Deuteronomy 32:44–47. What was Israel to do and why? Next, read the first and last chapters of Joshua; write down the key words you expect to emerge time and again throughout the book.

Based on your current understanding, how are the themes of *land* and *rest* fulfilled in Jesus Christ? What significance do these themes have for the Christian?

From what you know so far about the book of Joshua, what excites you? What confuses you? What questions do you hope to answer through this study?

As You Finish This Unit . . .

Take a few minutes to ask for God's help to grasp the story and significance of the book of Joshua, with all of its promises and commands. Ask for a clearer vision of the kind of Savior Christ is, the kind of people Christ saves, and the kind of salvation Christ brings.

Definitions

[1] **Eschatology** – Study of the end times as described in the Bible. Includes such topics as the return of Christ, the period of tribulation, the resurrection and judgment of all people, and the millennial reign of Christ on earth.

[2] **Covenant** – A binding agreement between two parties, typically involving a formal statement of their relationship, a list of stipulations and obligations for both parties, a list of witnesses to the agreement, and a list of curses for unfaithfulness and blessings for faithfulness to the agreement. The OT is more properly understood as the old covenant, meaning the agreement established between God and his people prior to the coming of Jesus Christ and the establishment of the new covenant (NT).

WEEK 2: AN OLD PROMISE, A NEW LEADER

Joshua 1:1-18

The first chapter of Joshua establishes the setting and agenda for the book. This chapter has been compared to the pistol shot at the beginning of a race, with all the action in the rest of the book starting from the people, commands, and promises introduced in this chapter. Of course, this chapter doesn't begin in isolation from the rest of the Bible's story. As we've considered, the book of Joshua is like the opening scene in a movie sequel. Here the characters and themes from the Pentateuch are carried forward. At the end of the Pentateuch, Moses died. This is where Joshua 1 begins.

The Big Picture

With Moses departed, the Lord commissions Joshua to lead his people into the land with courage and obedience to Moses' law—a daunting but achievable task, given the certainty of God's promises and presence.

> **Reflection and Discussion**

Read through Joshua 1:1–18, then engage this section of Scripture with the questions below. (For further background, see the *ESV Study Bible*, pages 394–395; available online at esv.org.)

1. God's Marching Orders for Joshua (1:1–9)

The first nine verses introduce a number of characters. Read these verses and write down the name of each character or group represented, along with what we learn about them. For background on Moses, read Deuteronomy 34.

Moses - disobedience
Joshua -
Hittites -
fore fathers
Israelites

Because of his sin against God (Numbers 20), Moses was not allowed to lead his people into the land. Now that Moses has died, God leads his people through Joshua. In a sentence, what is God commanding Joshua to do? What verse expresses the key to Joshua's success?

Joshua receives an order, and we have every reason to hear it as a difficult charge. How many times does God command Joshua, "Be strong and courageous"? What was there to fear? (See Numbers 13 for context.)

4 times he is told.
They were afraid because the people of Canaan were powerful, the cities fortified, and very large. Even giants lived there. descendents of anak

Joshua had good reasons to be afraid, but God gave him better reasons to be courageous. List the reasons God gave Joshua to be "strong and courageous." What is the main reason?

1) inherit land promised
2) to obey all the ~~way~~ law (don't turn to right or left
3) meditate on the law)
4) do not be afraid
God will be w/you wherever you go (Joshua) (He)

Num 32:1, 20-25,33

Having spent some time in the passage, we can't escape the presence of Moses. There are important points of continuity between God's dealing with his people under Joshua and under Moses. What assurances does this afford Joshua?

Deuteronomy 18:9-13
Genesis 15:16

2. Joshua's Marching Orders for the Nation (1:10–18)

The people of Israel would have been waiting their whole lives, quite literally, for this moment. What emotions do you think they experienced when Joshua's men gave the orders to begin preparations?

This chapter is specifically structured to communicate a certain logic about how God leads his people. How does God speak to and lead his people?

Throughout the book we'll encounter many easy-to-forget people. In 1:12, however, we meet a set of three tribes: "the Reubenites, the Gadites, and the half-tribe of Manasseh." Understanding their backstory will help us understand parts of this book. Read Numbers 32 and write down the reason these people have made a home east of the Jordan.

In Joshua's speech he uses an important word to interpret God's gift of land. What word does he use, and what do you suppose this means?

In light of the Bible's story to this point, what is surprising about the people's response in Joshua 1:16–18? For a comparison, read Numbers 14:36–38 for a summary of how the previous generation responded to the same task.

The chapter ends with another command to Joshua to "be strong and courageous" (Josh. 1:18), this time from the lips of the people. Courage is possible because of God's promise: "I will not leave you or forsake you" (1:5). How does Hebrews 13:5–6 apply this promise to Christians?

Read through the following *Gospel Glimpses, Whole-Bible Connections*, and *Theological Soundings*. Then take time to consider the *Personal Implications* these reflections have for your walk with the Lord.

Gospel Glimpses

"I WILL BE WITH YOU." It is remarkable that God would say something like this to a human being. It is true that God is present everywhere, but God promises to be with Joshua in a personal way. In the opening chapters of Scripture, God spoke with Adam and Eve and walked among them (Genesis 1–2). But Joshua lives on the other side of Genesis 3, where man is outside God's presence and under his wrath. This is why God's promise to be with Joshua—a promise made also to Abraham, to Moses, and later to David—is a sign of great hope for humanity. If God promised never to forsake Joshua, perhaps there is hope for us as well. And there is. In Christ, God dwelt among his people (Isa. 7:14; Matt. 1:23; John 1:14), and today the Lord is with us in an even more direct way through the Spirit (Matt. 28:20; 1 Cor. 3:16; 6:19).

"JUST AS I PROMISED." God owes us justice for our sin. Yet the Bible is a story that unfolds along a string of promises from God to us for our eternal good. In fact, God's promises are the connective tissue holding the whole story of the Bible together. In Genesis 3:15, God promised that a son of Eve would crush the head of the Serpent, who is Satan. In Joshua 1, his promise to be with Joshua is a promise of victory in the land of Canaan, a promise in continuity with his promise to Moses. In the course of this story we will see how God's promises work together in this book to prepare us to see how every Old Testament promise finds fulfillment in Jesus Christ (2 Cor. 1:20). God's faithfulness in this story strengthens our faith in his promises to us through Jesus.

Whole-Bible Connections

OBEDIENCE AND THE BOOK. Joshua 1:8 is a key verse for grasping the story of Joshua and its significance in the story of the Bible. The word "law" might call to mind the idea of civil law, or perhaps the commandments in Scripture. In Joshua, however, the "Book of the Law" refers to the five books of Moses: Genesis, Exodus, Leviticus, Numbers, and Deuteronomy. These books include commands, but much more. They instruct Israel in knowing and relating to God. Central to this is her relationship to God's leader. When the Lord instructed Moses concerning the kind of king Israel should seek, he gave a straightforward job description: ". . . he shall write for himself in a book a copy of this law. . . . and he shall read in it all the days of his life, that he may learn to fear the LORD his God by keeping all the words of this law, . . . that he may continue long in his kingdom, he and his children" (Deut. 17:18–20). For Joshua, careful obedience to God's law would be his path to success, and disobedience his undoing. Indeed, Christ will delight in God's law (compare Ps. 1:2), keeping it perfectly on our behalf.

A LEADER LIKE MOSES. Moses was a towering figure in the life of Israel. In Deuteronomy 34:9–11, Moses' unique status is highlighted: "There has not arisen a prophet since in Israel like Moses." Moses was the mediator of God's covenant with his people, and thus the people's fate was tied to his (Ex. 33:7–16). In the first chapter of Joshua he is mentioned 11 times, and Joshua's success is guaranteed with the promise that God would be with him "just as" he was with Moses (Josh. 1:3, 5, 17). Even more, it is by following the law that Joshua will have success (vv. 7–8) and will attain the land first promised to Moses (v. 3). Joshua will function as a new Moses, but he is not Moses' final successor. Jesus Christ is the greater Moses, a prophet superlative to Moses who reveals God fully, leads his people perfectly, and brings a better covenant (see Acts 3:22; Heb. 3:1–6; 8:6).

A PLACE OF REST. One of the Bible's most important images for salvation emerges in this chapter almost unnoticed: rest. Quoting Moses, Joshua says to the people, "The LORD your God is providing you a place of rest and will give you this land" (Josh. 1:13; see also Deut. 12:10). On the seventh day of creation, "God rested from all his work," entering into the full enjoyment of his creation (Gen. 2:2–3). For this reason the seventh day of the week was set apart as holy and as a pattern for mankind (Ex. 31:12–18). God promised rest in the land to Moses, and Moses promised the same to God's people: enjoyment of God in the place of his presence (Ex. 33:14; Deut. 3:20; 12:9; 25:19). With this as background, Jesus invites sinners to salvation with these words: "Come to me . . . and I will give you rest" (Matt. 11:28). Coming to Jesus is the only way to find true rest, since Jesus' saving work is the only means of favor with God (Heb. 4:10).

Theological Soundings

GOD HAS A NAME. It is hard to say we know someone if we don't know his or her name. For this reason, God has given us a name by which to call him. The name Yahweh, translated "LORD," is God's personal name. It is the name he used when he introduced himself to Moses from a burning bush, and it is how he intended to be remembered by his people: "Say this to the people of Israel: 'The LORD' . . . is my name forever, and thus I am to be remembered throughout all generations" (Ex. 3:15). God is committed to being known. This is why he called and covenanted with Abraham and his sons, and this is why he reveals himself to us with a name. As the Bible unfolds, God will be called a rock, a fortress, and many other descriptive names. But Yahweh, meaning "I am," is his proper and personal name. In covenant love he comes to Joshua, and this is how he comes to us.

GOD SPEAKS. The God of the Bible is a speaking God, which explains how we have a Bible. While God spoke through his leader, Joshua, time and again, this was largely to expound what Moses had *written*. In this way, Joshua's generation was the first to truly live *by the book*. The church[1] lives under a book as well, but according to the author of Hebrews, our position is much better: "Long ago, at many times and in many ways, God spoke to our fathers by the prophets, but in these last days he has spoken to us by his Son" (Heb. 1:1–2). Jesus sent his Spirit to inspire our New Testament Scriptures through his apostles[2] and prophets so that today the "word of Christ" dwells in us by means of his written Word (Col. 3:16; 2 Pet. 1:19; see also 2 Tim. 3:16; Heb. 4:12). This Word, says Peter, is more reliable than his own firsthand experience of Jesus' glorious transfiguration (2 Pet. 1:17–19).

> ## Personal Implications

Take time to reflect on the implications of Joshua 1:1–18 for your life. How does this passage lead you to praise God, repent of sin, and trust in his gracious promises? Write down your reflections under the three headings we have considered and on the passage as a whole.

1. Gospel Glimpses

2. Whole-Bible Connections

3. Theological Soundings

----

4. Joshua 1:1–18

> ## ▶ As You Finish This Unit . . .

For Joshua, courageous obedience would mean safety and success against his enemies. For Jesus, who sweat drops of blood on the night of his arrest, obedience would mean suffering in the place of his enemies under God's wrath. Praise God in prayer for the perfect obedience and suffering of Christ!

Definitions

[1] **Church** – From a Greek word meaning "assembly." The body of believers in Jesus Christ, referring either to all believers everywhere or to a local gathering of believers.

[2] **Apostle** – Means "one who is sent" and refers to one who is an official representative of another. In the NT, refers specifically to those whom Jesus chose to represent him.

Week 3: Sending in the Spies, Finding a Surprise

Joshua 2:1–24

The Place of the Passage

Israel has been here before. Forty years earlier, at the edge of the land, Moses sent in 12 spies to bring a report. The result was a disaster, not because of the intimidating reality beyond the Jordan but because of the faithless timidity of the spies who insisted Israel not go in. God had proven himself trustworthy, but his people would not trust him, and so that generation died in the wilderness. Now, 40 years later, Joshua secretly sends two spies. He trusts God, but perhaps he is not so trusting of men. Joshua does not send his spies to decide whether to enter the land but to decide *how* to enter. Their report is optimistic in ways he could not have imagined.

The Big Picture

Joshua sends two spies into Canaan, who return with a favorable report and a surprising story, confirming God's sovereignty[1] and hinting at his global purposes.

> ### Reflection and Discussion

Read through Joshua 2:1–24, then engage this section of Scripture with the questions below. (For further background, see the *ESV Study Bible*, pages 396–397; available online at esv.org.)

1. A Visit with a Prostitute (2:1–14)

One way the writer of Joshua draws attention to features in his story is through surprise. Surprises make up this chapter, although they may be obscured if you're familiar with the account. With an eye to these surprises, read verses 1–14 and list unexpected things that happen. Which surprise is most significant?

2 spies
Rahab

It seems suspect for Israel's spies to enter the home of a prostitute. Does the context suggest any wrongdoing? Why might it have been strategic to enter a prostitute's house?

Rahab's confession is probably the last thing these men expected. She is a female, Gentile prostitute in a Canaanite city. Read Rahab's confession in 2:9–13 and list everything you learn she believes about God. What does it tell us about Rahab's knowledge of Yahweh that she would appeal to these men for help?

2. A Sneaky Escape (2:15–24)

What surprises do you see in this second half of the story?

With the city gate closed behind them, the spies were no doubt relieved by Rahab's getaway plan. By her actions Rahab demonstrated her creativity and intelligence, but the most important thing about Rahab was her faith in Israel's God. How would you respond to someone who said, "I find it hard to believe that this Gentile prostitute really believes what she says. Where's the proof?"

actions : 23 proofed her faith
James 2

The spies' meeting Rahab was not accidental. What purpose does Rahab serve in God's plan of salvation? What do we learn from her about God's concern for the nations?

Prostitutes don't normally receive praise for their actions, yet Rahab did. What do her mentions in Matthew 1:5 and Hebrews 11:31 tell us about who God is and the kind of people he saves?

Read through the following *Gospel Glimpses, Whole-Bible Connections,* and *Theological Soundings*. Then take time to consider the *Personal Implications* these reflections have for your walk with the Lord.

Gospel Glimpses

GOD'S SURPRISING SOVEREIGNTY. This story is full of danger for Israel's spies. Jericho's king smelled blood, and only a prostitute stood between Israel's spies and the king's officials. The officials left the city, but then closed the gate behind them. This desperate situation, however, was actually quite positive. Jericho "melted" in fear (Josh. 2:11), but Rahab believed, showed them a window, and mapped their way home. Thus the spies were right to declare, "Truly the LORD has given all the land into our hands" (v. 24)—precisely what Rahab had already told them, in faith (vv. 8–9). If ever we're tempted to doubt the possibility that God can save this or that person, remember how God brought his spies home, and more importantly, how he brought this unlikely woman to himself.

DELIVERER FROM DEATH. Rahab knew her problem: she was a Canaanite, a sinner, and the object of God's coming judgment. She also knew her only hope: God's mercy. So, after a beautiful confession, Rahab pleaded for her life: "Please swear to me by the LORD that . . . you will . . . deliver our lives from death" (2:12–13). God didn't owe her for helping the spies, yet she asked for mercy—and God granted it, proving this truth: "everyone who calls on the name of the Lord will be saved" (Rom. 10:13). Nothing is more terrifying than death. No one is safer to trust than the Lord of life.

Whole-Bible Connections

SALVATION TO A GENTILE. When God came to Abraham, he gave him this promise: "In your offspring shall all the nations of the earth be blessed" (Gen. 22:18). Rahab was a Gentile, but by faith she became a child of Abraham (see Rom. 4:16), and so enjoyed an early installment of God's fulfillment of his promise to Abraham to extend his blessing to the nations. This is the way God works: the first believer in the land was a former Gentile marked for judgment, who would herself join the genealogy of Jesus Christ (Matt. 1:5).

FAITH AND WORKS. Rahab's story shows us the beautiful and interlocking relationship between faith and works. "By faith," writes the author of Hebrews, "Rahab the prostitute did not perish with those who were disobedient, because she had given a friendly welcome to the spies" (Heb. 11:31). Similarly, James

24

finds in Rahab an example of the inevitable expression of saving faith: "Was not also Rahab the prostitute justified by works when she received the messengers and sent them out by another way?" (James 2:25). How did Rahab's faith lead to these concrete actions? Based on what she had heard of Israel's God (Josh. 2:9–11), she considered herself safer helping the spies than turning them in, for—as far as she was concerned—the land was already theirs (v. 9). Her actions were driven by her faith. She hung the scarlet cord because she entrusted her life to God's mercy for salvation from the wrath to come. Salvation always comes to sinners by faith, and always produces good works (Rom. 4:1–5; James 2:21).

Theological Soundings

ONE TRUE GOD. Rahab gets it right when she says, "The LORD your God, he is God in the heavens above and on the earth beneath" (Josh. 2:11). Rahab's monotheism[2] is a great surprise and on the high point of this passage. The Canaanites were polytheistic, believing in myriad gods who were unjust, jealous, and in competition. They were takers, requiring even the sacrifice of children. According to the prophet Jeremiah, these idols, which are really nothing, "have to be carried, for they cannot walk. . . . The LORD is the true God" (Jer. 10:5, 10). Turning from false gods to the only true God is evidence of true salvation, just as it was for first-century Christians who "turned to God from idols to serve the living and true God" (1 Thess. 1:9).

HARDNESS OF UNBELIEF. Rahab's faith is such a prominent part of this story that we might miss an important lesson in the shadows of this passage. The men knocking at Rahab's door weren't there to plead for mercy. They knew of God's wonders but were there at the king's command to capture Israel's spies (Josh. 2:10–11). Surely, in Jericho's "melting" (see v. 11) we see a picture of the hardness of human sin. They knew and yet resisted God's power. In the salvation of Israel, Yahweh is going to bring judgment upon the people of Canaan, just as he said to Abraham 400 years before (Gen. 15:16). In God's perfect timing, God's judgment would come upon a people totally devoted to sin and unrelenting in their hardness of heart.

A FAITHFUL LIE? Some questions not raised directly by the text are nonetheless raised in our minds as we read Joshua 2. Was Rahab right to lie to the local officials? God's people are strictly prohibited from lying, yet the New Testament unblushingly commends Rahab as a model of faith (Heb. 11:31; James 2:25; see also Ex. 1:17–22; Heb. 11:23). What are we to make of this? First, narrative texts such as this may describe events without commending the actions in the story. Second, given Rahab's background, we should not be surprised at her decision under these circumstances. Third, it is fair to suggest that Rahab is playing by

25

rules appropriate for just warfare, deceiving with words just as camouflage does with cover. Whatever the case may be, we should be cautious in our application of texts like this. We should also be cautious not to miss the main point of the passage: the surprising faith of this unlikely character. Focusing on the main purpose of the text will provide the best interpretation and application.

Personal Implications

Take time to reflect on the implications of Joshua 2:1–24 for your life. How does this passage lead you to praise God, repent of sin, and trust in his gracious promises? Write down your reflections under the three headings we have considered and on the passage as a whole.

1. Gospel Glimpses

2. Whole-Bible Connections

3. Theological Soundings

4. Joshua 2:1–24

▶ **As You Finish This Unit . . .**

Praise God for his sovereignty to save sinners from among the nations, and pray for God's help to demonstrate your faith in Christ in the details of life.

Definitions

[1] **Sovereignty** – Supreme and independent power and authority. Sovereignty over all things is a distinctive attribute of God (1 Tim. 6:15–16). He directs all things to carry out his purposes (Rom. 8:28–29).

[2] **Monotheism** – The belief that there is only one true God. One of the distinguishing characteristics of the Israelites in the OT and of Christians, their spiritual heirs.

WEEK 4: CROSSING THE JORDAN, GETTING RIGHT WITH GOD

Joshua 3:1–5:15

▲

The Place of the Passage

The people of Israel got up in the morning and approached the Jordan River without any strategy for crossing except to obey Joshua and remember what God had done for their parents at the Red Sea. For three days they camped with the sound of floodwaters in their ears, the sight of the opposite shore reminding them of the mission ahead. For Joshua and the people, the experience of crossing the river would strengthen their dependence on the Lord and solidify their own place in God's redemptive story.

The Big Picture

At God's command, Joshua led the nation over the Jordan in a way that strengthened their dependence on the Lord and prepared them for what was ahead.

Reflection and Discussion

Read through Joshua 3:1–5:15, then engage with this section of Scripture using the questions below. (For further background, see the *ESV Study Bible*, pages 397–401; available online at esv.org.)

1. Witnessing God's Wonders (3:1–17)

On a human level, passing over the Jordan is impossible. Both the waters and what is on the other side present a grave threat to Israel's life. List the features of this story that add a sense of impossibility.

The ark of the covenant was not a magic charm that allowed Israel to do miraculous things. The ark represented God's presence among his people. It was a symbol of his great holiness, as well as his grace and nearness. What is the ark's function in this episode (see 3:10–13)?

At one level, God's purpose in performing this miracle is to move his people into the land. But twice in this passage we have an indication of God's more significant purpose. What is this purpose?

What wonder has God performed for the Christian, and how does this advance the same purpose for his people today?

2. Declaring God's Mighty Hand (4:1–24)

Chapter 4 begins when "all the nation had finished passing over the Jordan," yet the Lord still holds back the water for a time. In fact, all of chapter 4 takes place at the riverbank. There the Lord gives instructions for a memorial. At the end of the chapter, two purposes are expressed for this memorial, one each for two different groups. Who are these two groups, and what is the Lord's purpose for each?

What does the provision of this memorial tell us about God? What does the need for this memorial reveal about human nature?

In 4:14 we hear an echo from a verse in chapter 3. What verse is it? What does the repetition of this statement tell us about how God chooses to bring salvation?

Joshua 3:10 reveals God's purpose in leading his people using the ark of the covenant. What does chapter 4 reveal about God's purpose for the nations through this event?

3. Living and Leading on God's Terms (5:1–15)

Now that the nation has passed over the Jordan, we might expect an immediate move on Jericho. Instead, several things must happen first. The first order of business is circumcision,[1] a covenantal imperative that had been neglected by this generation. Based on Joshua 5:9, how would you express the purpose of circumcision for Israel (see also Gen. 17:10–14 and Deut. 30:5–6)?

A second order of business involves another symbol given to Israel: the Passover. Read Exodus 12:1–14, 26–28. Answering with one sentence for each question, what was the Passover event, and why did the Lord want them to remember it?

At the end of this chapter we meet an unnamed man. This is likely the same figure mentioned to Moses by the Lord in Exodus 23:20–23 and 33:1–3. What indications do we have in Joshua 5:13–15 of this man's identity? Given the placement of this story between the crossing of the Jordan and the movement toward Jericho, what point is God making to Joshua and to us?

Humanly speaking, Joshua and the people had everything to fear: cutting-edge military technology, trained and determined armies, and walled cities built for war. But because of what God had done for them, and the presence of the Lord's commander, they had every reason to trust his promises for what was ahead. Read Romans 8:31–38. On what basis can we trust God's promises for the future? What do you need courage for today? Write out a brief prayer asking God to give you courage to stay faithful.

Read through the following *Gospel Glimpses, Whole-Bible Connections,* and *Theological Soundings.* Then take time to consider the *Personal Implications* these reflections have for your walk with the Lord.

Gospel Glimpses

THE LORD WILL DO WONDERS. What must the people of Israel have felt when Joshua said, "Consecrate yourselves, for tomorrow the LORD will do wonders among you" (Josh. 3:5)? With no means of getting across the Jordan, they could nonetheless imagine how this might go. The Lord did "wonders" for their parents' generation when he struck Egypt and parted the Red Sea (Ex. 3:20). Now it was their turn. Yet these wonders would not fix Israel's problem of sin. More daunting than the Jordan is the human heart. Yet, for believers the spiritual wonder at work in us is more spectacular than anything Israel would ever see with their eyes. The power that raised Jesus from the dead has raised us and now works in us (Eph. 1:19–23).

REMEMBERING REDEMPTION. How kind is God to redeem us *and* bring to our remembrance what he has done! As God commanded Moses to lead his people out of Egypt, he gave him instructions for how this redemption was to be remembered in the Passover meal (Exodus 12). For Joshua's generation, 12 stones will help them tell their story. For new covenant Christians, Jesus instituted the Lord's Supper to represent his body and blood, saying, "Do this in remembrance of me" (Luke 22:19; see also 1 Cor. 11:25–26). Likewise, baptism pictures our union with Christ in his death, burial, and resurrection (Rom. 6:3–4). The Lord knows our need and has graciously given us these symbols to remind us of our redemption.

33

> ## Whole-Bible Connections

PATTERNS OF PROMISE THAT LEAD TO CHRIST. What do circumcision, the ark of the covenant, the Passover, and the land have to do with the New Testament Christian? They lead us to Christ by clarifying our need for, and the nature of, the salvation he brings. The Passover prepared God's people to receive Christ as their substitute (1 Cor. 5:7). Circumcision reminded them they needed a change that was more than skin-deep (see Deut. 10:16 and 30:6)—only through Jesus Christ's circumcision could the foreskin of their hearts be made clean (Phil. 3:3; Col. 2:11). The ark created a longing for true access to God, which came when Jesus dwelt among us, and in greater measure through the Spirit who now dwells in believers (John 1:14; 14:6). These may be some of the things Jesus explained to his disciples when, "beginning with Moses and all the Prophets, he interpreted to them in all the Scriptures the things concerning himself" (Luke 24:27).

COVENANT AS THE PROMISE STRUCTURE OF SCRIPTURE. By grasping the internal structure of the Bible's story we can understand exactly how Joshua's patterns lead us to Christ and transform our lives. God's salvation story is revealed through a series of progressively unfolding covenant promises: covenants with Noah and creation, with Abraham and his sons, with Moses and Israel, and with David and his future Son. Each of these covenants carries forward God's original purpose for his creation and his promise to redeem humanity and destroy Satan (Genesis 1–3), and each of these covenants is fulfilled in the coming of a new covenant in Jesus Christ (Jer. 31:31–34; Luke 22:20). The Sinaitic Covenant (sometimes called the Mosaic covenant), which provides the context for Joshua, includes commandments, provisions, and patterns preparing God's people to understand their need for a messianic leader. While Joshua would eventually bring Israel into the land, once in the land it became evident Joshua was not their final savior. Sin still plagued Israel, and Joshua would die. What Israel needed was a faithful covenant mediator who would win for them through obedience the blessing God explained to Moses, taking the curse that was theirs because of sin (see Gal. 3:13). As the New Testament puts it, "The law has but a shadow of the good things to come"; it was "our guardian until Christ came" (Heb. 10:1; Gal. 3:24; see also Matt. 5:17). Joshua is a wonderful example of how the Sinaitic Covenant functioned in ancient Israel and prepared the way for the final covenant Jesus would establish.

THAT ISRAEL MAY KNOW; THAT THE EARTH MAY KNOW. We should not miss the clear statements of purpose in this story. God leads with the ark so that Israel "shall know that the living God is among" them (Josh. 3:10–13); he leads his people across the Jordan as he had through the Red Sea "so that all the peoples of the earth may know that the hand of the LORD is mighty" (4:24). This dual purpose—for Israel and for the earth—was at work when David decapitated Goliath: "that all the earth may know that there is a God in Israel, and that all this assembly may know that the LORD saves not with sword and spear. For the battle is the LORD's" (1 Sam. 17:46–47). Worldwide witness to God's glory was why the Lord raised up Pharaoh 40 years before (Ex. 19:6), and it is what the prophets look forward to in the new creation (Hab. 2:14). While Adam's race failed to fill the earth with God's glory, the promised One would be a light to the nations (Isa. 49:6). Thus, while Israel's life was centered in the land and, later, in Jerusalem, this was only temporary. Before his ascension, Jesus sent his disciples from Jerusalem to the ends of the earth (Acts 1:8), because—as God always intended—the knowledge of his glory must cover the entire earth.

Theological Soundings

THEY STOOD IN AWE OF HIM. One thing we cannot escape, in reading the book of Joshua, is the centrality of Joshua to everything God does for his people. When God speaks and leads, he does so through Joshua, just as he did through Moses. Of course, Joshua will die, just as Moses died. And when he does, Israel will need another leader. And for Israel, as for us, there is the promise of One to come who will surpass both Joshua and Moses: "The LORD your God will raise up for you a prophet like me from among you . . . —it is to him you shall listen" (Deut. 18:15). If the people stood in awe of Joshua, how much more shall we stand in awe of the risen Christ! Such a sense of awe is the true goal of theological reflection and the study of Scripture.

A COMMANDER, AND THE PREINCARNATE CHRIST. We have good reason to believe that the nameless man that appeared to Joshua is the preincarnate[2] Son of God. He is divine, since Joshua worships him without rebuke, and yet he is distinct from the Lord who speaks to Joshua. Clarity comes with the progress of revelation. The Son of God was the Father's agent in creating the world (John 1:1–3; Col. 1:16–20; Heb. 1:1–3) and in redemption (Rom. 5:12–21; Eph. 1:7–12; Col. 1:13), and it appears that he was also the means of rescuing Israel from Egypt (see Jude 5). By appearing to Joshua at this moment, God is saying, "I'll take care of this." This commander does not deal with Joshua on Joshua's terms, but confronts Joshua with a sword drawn. Allied with God's commander through obedience to God's Word, Joshua and his mission cannot fail.

Personal Implications

Take time to reflect on the implications of Joshua 3:1–5:15 for your life. How does this passage lead you to praise God, repent of sin, and trust in his gracious promises? Write down your reflections under the three headings we have considered and on the passage as a whole.

1. Gospel Glimpses

2. Whole-Bible Connections

3. Theological Soundings

4. Joshua 3:1–5:15

As You Finish This Unit . . .

Thank God in prayer for the wonder of the gospel and the symbols by which we remember and proclaim what God has done: the Lord's Supper and baptism. Pray for God's people to fear him, and his mighty hand to be known throughout the earth.

Definitions

[1] **Circumcision** – The ritual practice of removing the foreskin of an individual, which was commanded for all male Israelites in OT times as a sign of participation in the covenant God established with Abraham (Gen. 17:9–14).

[2] **Incarnation** – Literally "[becoming] in flesh," it refers to God becoming a human being in the person of Jesus of Nazareth.

Week 5: A Foolish Plan, a Decisive Outcome

Joshua 6:1–27

▲

It is difficult to imagine which obstacle would be more intimidating: the flood-swollen Jordan, or Jericho. Having witnessed the wonders of God's parting the Jordan, Israel should have every reason to trust that the Lord is with Joshua as they approach Jericho (Josh. 3:7). In chapter 6 all eyes are on this fortified city, a city built for a fight and filled with men trained for war. But this city, as the spies found out, was melting in fear (2:11), fully aware of Yahweh's power. The God of Israel was the God of heaven and earth, and he had a claim on Jericho. The manner in which the Lord took this city was carefully tuned to make a point, both to the surrounding peoples and to Israel.

The Big Picture

The author gives us a play-by-play telling of Jericho's capture, a story carefully designed to make a point about God's promises and how he brings them to fulfillment.

> ## Reflection and Discussion

Read through Joshua 6:1–27, then reflect on this section of Scripture using the questions below. (For further background, see the *ESV Study Bible*, pages 401–403; available online at esv.org.)

1. Joshua Receives the Battle Plan (6:1–5)

Throughout the book of Joshua we hear a cadence of commands—and promises making them possible. In 6:1–5, what does God promise? What does he command?

As this book unfolds, the ark of the covenant is consistently in the middle of the action. How would you explain the role of the ark in Israel's life? What implication does this have for the moral legitimacy of Israel's invasion and destruction of these Canaanite cities?

2. Joshua Carries Out the Battle Plan (6:6–27)

This chapter builds suspense, especially when Joshua tells the people to shout (vv. 16–20). Just before they shout, Israel receives a set of commands. What is the significance of the timing of these commands?

Joshua's victory at Jericho is total. List every indication, in the story, of Joshua's complete victory. Then, read Genesis 15:12–21 and state one reason for the totality and timing of this battle.

The nation has crossed the Jordan and taken Jericho with perfect success. How should the people of Israel and the reader of the story respond to this success?

Joshua 6:21 is difficult for some readers. The destruction of men, women, children, the elderly, and animals should sober us as we read. Thankfully, we may trust God's Word at every point without grasping fully why God says or does what he does. Assuredly God is good (Ps. 119:68) and just (Gen. 18:25), and his Word proves true (Prov. 30:5; Ps. 12:6). What is your best explanation for why God is just in issuing these orders? Several passages may be helpful in working this out, including Genesis 1:1; 15:15–16; Deuteronomy 9:5; 20:10–18; and Leviticus 18:24–25; 20:1–5.

In Hebrews 11:30–31, two feats of faith are mentioned—one carried out by Israel and another by a Gentile. What do these parties have in common?

First Corinthians 1:18–31 describes salvation through Christ similarly to how we might describe salvation at Jericho. Read that passage and answer these questions: How does God save? Whom does God save? Why does God save in this way?

Read through the following *Gospel Glimpses, Whole-Bible Connections,* and *Theological Soundings*. Then take time to consider the *Personal Implications* these reflections have for your walk with the Lord.

Gospel Glimpses

GRACE OF GOD. God alone deserves credit for this victory at Jericho. The marching, trumpets, and shouting by themselves would accomplish nothing. It was the Lord who made Jericho fear, and it was the Lord who made her walls fall. And yet, what Christ accomplished for sinners through his death and resurrection is infinitely more profound and humanly impossible than what we witness here. As we consider our own salvation in Christ, we can take no credit for it. In Ephesians 1 the apostle Paul reflects on the spiritual blessings that come to us through Christ, including predestination, adoption, redemption, forgiveness, and the indwelling of the Holy Spirit. These blessings come from the Father (Eph. 1:3–6), Son (vv. 7–12), and Spirit (vv. 13–14), and each blessing is given to magnify the praise of God's glorious grace (vv. 6, 12, 14). From the beginning to the end of our salvation, God does the work, so that our boast is in him alone (Rom. 11:36; 1 Cor. 1:31; Eph. 1:8–9; 2:8–9).

GOD'S FOOLISH PLAN TO SAVE. To any human observer, Joshua's plan for battle was utterly ridiculous—but it was not Joshua's plan. Given to him by Yahweh himself (Josh. 6:2–5), Joshua's battle plan amplified God's wisdom, not man's. The Lord could have flattened the city ahead of Israel's arrival, but he did it like this to confound human wisdom and demonstrate his strength. The apparent folly of God's salvation strategies is even more profound at the cross. There Jesus Christ died to flatten the fortified city of sin and death and hell. For, in the cross, "God chose what is foolish in the world to shame the wise; God chose what is weak in the world to shame the strong; . . . so that no human being might boast in the presence of God" (1 Cor. 1:27, 31).

Whole-Bible Connections

"DEVOTED FOR DESTRUCTION." Suspense builds across the chapter leading to Israel's "shout." After receiving instructions concerning the shout, Joshua gives the instructions to shout and commands the people to do so. But before they can give their shout, Joshua speaks to them about things that are to be "devoted to destruction" (Josh. 6:17–21). This was not an oversight remembered at the last minute. Its placement highlights its importance. The point of total destruction was to signal to Israel that this invasion and this place were not theirs but the Lord's (Deut. 20:10–18). This was not an imperialistic human invasion but a divine judgment. When we come to the New Testament, we see the battle moved to the realm of the unseen. Through his resurrection, Jesus is now exalted over *every* unseen power and enemy of God (Eph. 1:20–22), and he empowers his people for battle against these forces (6:10–20). Likewise, the new creation will be cleansed of all evil (Rev. 21:8).

TOTAL OBEDIENCE FOR A TOTAL VICTORY. When the walls fell down, they "fell down flat" (Josh. 6:20). When Israel took the city, they "devoted all in the city to destruction" (v. 21). And as if that were not enough, after rescuing Rahab, "they burned the city with fire, and everything in it" (v. 24), and Joshua put a curse on anyone "who rises up and builds this city" (v. 26)—a judgment that would actually be fulfilled several hundred years later (see 1 Kings 16:34). An exception to Israel's obedience will play out in the chapter ahead, but the lesson learned here is how God keeps his promise of blessing for obedience. Just as God promised in Joshua 1:8, Joshua's law-keeping brought military success. In this way, Jericho serves as a paradigm for every future battle that Israel would face in the Old Testament. Moreover, in the New Testament, Jesus Christ, a second Joshua, wins the victory by means of keeping God's law perfectly (Heb. 10:5–10) and defeating his enemies with his own counterintuitive military operation—namely, the incarnation and crucifixion (Heb. 2:14–15).

Theological Soundings

JOSHUA'S SWORD AND THE JUSTICE OF GOD. In Joshua's hand there is a sword covered with the blood of women and children. We should be careful not to measure God's justice by our own standards (Deut. 32:4). We are finite and fallen in our understanding. Yet thoughtful readers will wonder why God would command this slaughter. This is difficult, but let us consider what we know from Scripture. First, God is the creator and therefore the owner of all things. Life is his to make or take (Deut. 32:39; 1 Sam. 2:6). Second, we were created to glorify God, but every human is born guilty, corrupt, and condemned under sin (see Rom. 5:12–21). This is the reason that everyone eventually dies. Third, as with many aspects of Israel's life under the old covenant, there are many foreshadowings of future realities, including salvation but also judgment. Here, as in Noah's generation, God brings that future sentence into the present. Thus God's conquest of Canaan is not a model for us to imitate but a pattern of God's final judgment in hell.[1] Fourth, the Lord was patient with the Canaanites, having allowed generations for the sin of this people—which included child sacrifice—to come to full flower (Gen. 15:16; Lev. 18:24–26; 20:1–5; Deut. 9:5). Rahab's story highlights God's purpose to save anyone who finally turned to faith. Fifth, as a new Eden, the land was a sacred space for a "kingdom of priests and a holy nation" (Ex. 19:6; see also Lev. 18:24–25; Rev. 21:8). This explains why God's commands for total destruction were confined to the boundaries of Canaan (Deut. 20:10–18), and why Israel would be likewise judged if she fell to the same sin (Lev. 18:26–28; Deut. 28:25–68). Removing the unrepentant guarded Israel's purity (Deut. 7:3–4; 12:29–31). For all these reasons, this was not a human invasion for ethnic cleansing but a divine invasion for judgment and salvation (Deut. 32:43), a dramatic portrayal of what is required for God to be with man. Today, Christians wield a sword heavier and more severe than anything Joshua's army carried. Jesus' cross is covered in blood as well, and it covers our sins through faith (Rom. 3:25). But apart from faith, the gospel of the cross also warns of eternal judgment for sin (Rom. 1:16–18).

STUBBORNNESS OF SIN. The Lord gave Abraham a timeline for Israel's move into the land: "the iniquity of the Amorites is not yet complete" (Gen. 15:16). The completion finally came, and Joshua 6 is what it looked like. The depravity[2] of the human race is exemplified in the stubbornness of this Canaanite city. Certain of the power of Israel's God, after six whole days they would not bow to him. This is a picture of the condition of every human heart. Knowing our sin, apart from God's grace we still refuse to turn to him.

> ## Personal Implications

Take time to reflect on the implications of Joshua 6:1–27 for your life. How does this passage lead you to praise God, repent of sin, and trust in his gracious promises? Write down your reflections under the three headings we have considered and on the passage as a whole.

1. Gospel Glimpses

2. Whole-Bible Connections

3. Theological Soundings

4. Joshua 6:1–27

As You Finish This Unit . . .

Humble yourself before God in prayer, recognizing your salvation from a greater enemy than Jericho and by means even more foolish than a shout. Boast in the Lord alone for his grace and the foolishness of his cross.

Definitions

[1] **Hell** – A place of eternal torment for those who rebel against God and refuse to repent.

[2] **Depravity** – The sinful condition of human nature apart from grace, whereby humans are inclined to serve their own will and desires and to reject God's rule.

WEEK 6:
TWO PILES OF STONES,
ONE CRUCIAL LESSON

Joshua 7:1–8:35

The Place of the Passage

Chapter 7 comes as a shock. It opens with these ominous words: "But the people of Israel broke faith in regard to the devoted things" (v. 1). This will be a more complicated journey than chapter 6 may have led us to expect. The complicating factor is sin in the camp. One man disobeyed Joshua's instructions, the Lord burned with anger against the people, and the people bore the consequences. The story that follows is tragic but yields important lessons for Israel and for us. In these chapters we grasp the seriousness and consequences of sin, a prerequisite for grasping the gospel of grace—the good news to which this story ultimately points.

The Big Picture

Israel experiences the wrath of God for disobedience, and restoration of blessing for the obedience they learned.

> ### Reflection and Discussion

Read through Joshua 7:1–8:35, then consider this section of Scripture, following the questions below. (For further background, see the *ESV Study Bible*, pages 403–407; available online at esv.org.)

1. A Pile of Stones (7:1–26)

The chapter begins with a sober indication of sin's presence in Israel. Because of one man's sin, "the anger of the LORD burned against the people of Israel" (7:1). Put this statement about God's anger in your own words. How can God be angry with all the people of Israel for the sin of one Israelite?

We are given the backstory of why Israel failed at Ai, but Joshua didn't have the whole story yet. What do you make of Joshua's response in 7:7–9? Was Joshua's confusion and despair justified?

This chapter has a very clear structure, moving from setting, conflict, climax, to resolution. As the story grows in tension, what is its climax?

God's response to Achan may seem harsh, given Achan's specific sin. But this was much more than a small theft. Go back through the chapter and list the various descriptions of Achan's sin.

We may be able to hide our sin from others, but sin is never hidden from God. Identify indications from this chapter of the Lord's perfect and complete knowledge.

Even if coveting isn't a regular part of our vocabulary, Achan's desires are none-theless a regular part of our lives. Recall again Hebrews 13:5–6: what is the deeper problem behind our covetousness? What sins of covetousness come to mind for you when reading this chapter?

Achan clearly confessed his sin, but the broader context of Achan's confession, including its timing and what he didn't say, is not encouraging. What features of this account highlight the problem in Achan's heart?

Joshua 7:1 and 7:26 bookend the chapter with a contrast. What happened that changed the Lord's posture toward his people?

----

2. Another Pile of Stones (8:1–35)

In this story, two piles of stones are better than one! What is the significance of pairing the story in chapter 7 with the story in chapter 8?

Israel conquered Ai but took the king alive and proceeded to hang him before burying him under the heap of stones. We will see such action again in the next few chapters. Do you think it was appropriate? Why or why not?

With the drama of the last two chapters in mind, what is the purpose of the closing scene in 8:30–35?

Read through the following *Gospel Glimpses, Whole-Bible Connections,* and *Theological Soundings.* Then take time to consider the *Personal Implications* these reflections have for your walk with the Lord.

Gospel Glimpses

THE LORD'S PATIENCE. Joshua's response to Israel's failure at Ai is unreasonable, given all he knew of God. Previously he saw God bless his people with victory for obedience, and he knew well God's threat of defeat for unbelief. Based on Yahweh's covenantal relationship with Israel, Joshua should have discerned there was sin in their midst. Instead, in lament he appears to accuse God not only of failing his people but also of ill will toward them. Joshua sounds like Israel grumbling in the wilderness (see Ex. 16:3). The Lord's response is stern but appropriate: "Get up! Why have you fallen on your face? Israel has sinned" (Josh. 7:10–11). This rebuke is less than Joshua deserves and demonstrates the patience of our Lord—patience made possible because of Christ's future sacrifice[1] for such sins (Rom. 3:25).

GOD'S WORD, OUR LIFELINE. In the closing scene of chapter 8 we see Joshua gathering the people of Israel around God's Word. Every feature of this scene contributes to a sense of solemnity and worship: an altar of uncut stones, offerings, writing of the law, the standing positions of those present, and the reading of the law before the people. And when Joshua read the law, "There was not a word of all that Moses commanded that Joshua did not read before all the assembly of Israel" (Josh. 8:35). Such devotion to the law demonstrates what was also true for Christ and for us: "Man shall not live by bread alone, but by every word that comes from the mouth of God" (Deut. 8:3; Matt. 4:4).

Whole-Bible Connections

ONE MAN, CORPORATE GUILT. That God would burn with anger toward all of his people for the sin of one man may catch us off guard, but we should not be surprised. When Adam sinned, he plunged the entire human race into sin, with all of its guilt and death and condemnation (Rom. 5:12–14). This reality of corporate guilt is important for understanding how God relates to humanity. In judgment, God curses his people because of the sin of one man; but by the same token, in salvation God makes many sinners righteous through the obedience of one man (Rom. 5:15–19; 1 Cor. 15:22).

ISRAELITE IN NAME ONLY. Rahab appeared to be outside God's promise, but her faith proved her to be an insider. The opposite was true for Achan. He is not alone in Scripture. Judas betrayed Jesus for money (Luke 22:4–5). Many

49

who followed Jesus for bread would eventually turn away (John 6:26, 66). Even some who have called Jesus "Lord" will be surprised in the end (Matt. 7:21–23). Jesus used the imagery of different soils to help his disciples discern the various responses to his word (Mark 4:1–20). Here's what John said about those who abandon their faith: "If they had been of us, they would have continued with us. But they went out, that it might become plain that they all are not of us" (1 John 2:19). Those who belong to Christ will stay with Christ until the end, and their love for him will endure (Phil. 1:6; Heb. 3:14; 1 John 2:15–17).

▶ Theological Soundings

WRATH OF GOD. Chapter 7 is bookended with references to God's anger, highlighting its centrality to this section. The wrath of God is one of his divine attributes,[2] an emotion and action arising from his holiness and love for what is just and good. Wrath is not intrinsic to God's character, as love is, for without rebellion there is no wrath. What Achan gets in a pile of stones is what we deserve as sinners like him. We are born "children of wrath" (Eph. 2:3), and it is this fury of God's anger against human sin that Jesus suffered for us on the cross.

THE LORD'S PERFECT KNOWLEDGE. The Lord's slow but deliberate uncovering of Achan's sin is a reminder of the way his perfect knowledge exposes our secret thoughts and deeds (Ps. 44:21; Heb. 4:12). It should sober us that the Lord saw Achan when no one else did, for indeed a day is coming when God will judge "the secrets of men" (Rom. 2:16). It should sober us still more that Achan hid until his hand was forced. In love with darkness, men avoid the light; but on the promise of mercy and cleansing, the gospel invites Christian and non-Christian alike to confess sin and find forgiveness through the shed blood of Jesus Christ (1 John 1:9–2:2).

▶ Personal Implications

Take time to reflect on the implications of Joshua 7:1–8:35 for your life. How does this passage lead you to praise God, repent of sin, and trust in his gracious promises? Write down your reflections under the three headings we have considered and on the passage as a whole.

1. Gospel Glimpses

---

2. Whole-Bible Connections

3. Theological Soundings

4. Joshua 7:1–8:35

As You Finish This Unit . . .

Confess in prayer to God any sins that you have been hiding, recognizing he knows all things and will judge even our secrets. Then praise him for the cross, where Jesus suffered that judgment for even the most secret sins of those whose faith is in him.

Definitions

[1] **Sacrifice** – An offering to God, often to seek forgiveness of sin. The law of Moses gave detailed instructions regarding various kinds of sacrifices. By his death on the cross, Jesus gave himself as a sacrifice to atone for the sins of believers (Eph. 5:2; Heb. 10:12). Believers are to offer their bodies as living sacrifices to God (Rom. 12:1).

[2] **Attributes of God** – The distinctive characteristics of God as he is described in the Bible. These include eternality, faithfulness, goodness, graciousness, holiness, immutability, infinitude, justice, love, mercy, omnipotence, omnipresence, omniscience, self-existence, self-sufficiency, sovereignty, and wisdom.

WEEK 7:
TAKING MORE LAND,
HANGING MORE KINGS

Joshua 9:1–12:24

▲

Israel's experiences at Jericho and at Ai are a paradigm for interpreting the outcomes of all of their future victories or defeats. Achan's sin brought humility and self-suspicion on Israel's part; Jericho and the eventual victory at Ai brought great encouragement. After an interesting episode with some slick characters, this section amounts to a blitz across Canaan, a compressed account of victory after victory. These chapters of conquest bring us to the conclusion of the first half of the book, after which we read about the settling of the land.

The Big Picture

Joshua's conquest of the land winds down to a close, but not without a twist and another magnificent demonstration of the Lord's fighting for his people.

> **Reflection and Discussion**

Read through Joshua 9:1–12:24, then study this section of Scripture using the questions below. (For further background, see the *ESV Study Bible*, pages 408–415; available online at esv.org.)

1. The Gibeonites Bring Crumbly Bread (9:1–27)

This chapter is one big contrast. Who is the contrast between? How are they alike, and how are they different? What do we learn about the Gibeonites in 10:2 that adds to the drama?

Israel is victorious in the face of direct assault, but vulnerable to deception. Joshua knew the prohibition against making a covenant with the Canaanites (Deut. 7:2) and did not show proper caution. What does Joshua 9:14 reveal about Joshua's deeper problem?

Given all the stories that could be told of Joshua's conquests, why do you suppose this story was included (see Deut. 7:2 and Joshua 2)?

2. Five Kings Hang from Trees (10:1–43)

Chapter 10 ends with this summary: "The LORD God . . . fought for Israel" (10:42). List the ways God fought for Israel. Although unmentioned, what character from earlier in the story is responsible for these victories?

We have read numerous indications of God's purpose to exalt Joshua. Here again, as with the king of Ai, Joshua dramatically slays these kings (10:24–27). How might God's promise to the Serpent in Genesis 3:15 inform Joshua's method of execution?

In Joshua 10:28 the narrative picks up speed. What words or phrases are repeated? What's the significance of this repetition?

3. Joshua Finishes the Job and Takes Inventory (11:1–12:24)

Joshua 11:4–5 describes armies gathered "like the sand that is on the seashore." This imagery will be used to describe future battles in Scripture, including

WEEK 7: TAKING MORE LAND, HANGING MORE KINGS

history's final battle before God's final judgment (see Judg. 7:12; 1 Sam. 13:5; Rev. 20:8). What is this image intended to convey?

In Joshua 11:15 we read a familiar verb, repeated here three times. What key verse from chapter 1 stands behind this verse?

Joshua 11:20 gives us new insight into Israel's battles: "It was the LORD's doing to harden their hearts that they should come against Israel in battle." Does this mean that the Canaanites were like puppets, controlled by God and therefore without personal guilt?[1] What indications from Scripture lead you to answer this way?

Joshua 11:23 closes the first half of the book on a good note, indicating that the "land had rest from war." Yet verse 22 speaks of inhabitants that remain. Based on Moses' teaching, what are we to conclude about Israel from their unfinished work?

Chapter 12 is a detailed inventory of every place and king taken by Israel under Moses (12:1–6) and Joshua (vv. 7–24). While these people and places are unfamiliar to us, what would this catalog have represented to an ancient Israelite reader of this book?

Read through the following *Gospel Glimpses, Whole-Bible Connections*, and *Theological Soundings*. Then take time to consider the *Personal Implications* these reflections have for your walk with the Lord.

Gospel Glimpses

CRUMBLY BREAD FOR AN UNBREAKABLE COVENANT. The story of the Gibeonite deception can make us scratch our heads. They are an entertaining bunch, but who are these people, and what are they doing in the story? An important purpose emerges as we consider the parallels between these Gibeonites and Rahab: both are Canaanites set apart for destruction; both have heard about and fear Israel and her God; both know they are doomed unless they are accepted by Israel; both plead for mercy, albeit in a suspect and clumsy fashion; both are received and integrated into the covenant community. So it appears that God, even through Israel's foolish failings, is working out his plan (Deut. 7:2; Josh. 9:14). As promised, God is extending the blessing of Abraham to the nations (Gen. 12:1–3), a blessing fulfilled ultimately in the church.

FEARLESS BECAUSE THE LORD IS A FIGHTER. The Lord has not called Joshua to lead Israel in a merely human battle fought by merely human means. He uses his people, but he also throws stones and stops the sun (Josh. 10:11–13). For this reason, Joshua reminds the people, "Do not be afraid or dismayed; be strong and courageous. For thus the LORD will do to all your enemies against whom you fight" (Josh. 10:25). Christians can have this same confidence in the face of sin, death, and the Devil, because Jesus Christ suffered God's hail-throwing wrath that we deserve. The author of Hebrews tells us Jesus came so that "through death he might destroy the one who has the power of death, that is, the devil" (Heb. 2:14). Because of Christ's death, we can be fearless in the face of our own death, for Jesus has dealt decisively with our guilt before God as a "merciful and faithful high priest," suffering God's wrath against our sin (Heb. 2:17).

Whole-Bible Connections

FEET AND NECKS. Joshua's method for killing kings is deliberate and symbolic. These kings rule Canaanite outposts of Satan. In Genesis 3:15 God promised the Serpent that a son of Eve "shall bruise your head, and you shall bruise his heel." With the feet of Joshua's men on the necks of these kings, Satan gets a taste of what will come when Jesus Christ puts "all his enemies under his feet" (1 Cor. 15:25; see also Eph. 1:20–23). Adam himself was given "dominion" over the world, and in Joshua we see the exercise of God's dominion through Joshua. This conquering hero foreshadows the dominion Christ will ultimately exercise when all things are put under his feet (1 Cor. 15:26; Rev. 20:14; 21:8).

REST FROM WAR. In chapter 1, Joshua quoted Moses in speaking to the people: "The Lord your God is providing you a place of rest and will give you this land" (Josh. 1:13). Now, at the conclusion of the battle we read, "And the land had rest from war" (11:23). By way of reminder, "rest" has deep theological significance, reaching back to the seventh day, when God rested from creation, and forward to the Sabbath rest coming to believers in and through Christ (Gen. 2:2–3; Heb. 4:1–11).

Theological Soundings

HAILSTONES AND MIRACLES.[2] With stunning regularity the world works according to God's providential designs; however, God is pleased at times to break that regularity to demonstrate his sovereign rule. Miracles may present a difficulty for some, but the acceptance of miracles is basic to Christianity and to any reading of Scripture that honors it as God's Word. God is the creator; everything else is his creation. As Psalm 115:3 tells us, "Our God is in the heavens; he does all that he pleases." This includes hurling hailstones on his enemies and stopping the sun in the sky (Josh. 10:11, 13), miraculous acts of providence preparing the way for the virgin birth and Jesus' resurrection from the dead.

SOVEREIGNTY AND RESPONSIBILITY. Joshua 11:20 gives us new insight into Joshua's victory over his enemies: the Lord "harden[ed] their hearts." The apostle Paul answers a common question regarding God's absolute sovereignty and man's real responsibility: "Is there injustice on God's part? By no means! . . . He has mercy on whomever he wills, and he hardens whomever he wills" (Rom. 9:14–18). The Lord hardened Pharaoh's heart to demonstrate his power and proclaim his name (Rom. 9:17). Though mysterious, this hardening is not incompatible with human responsibility, for just as the Lord holds Pharaoh culpable, so he holds these Canaanites guilty for their sin (see Lev. 20:1–5; Deut. 9:5). By hardening the hearts of those whose hearts are already set against him, the Lord allows the full extent of human sinfulness to show itself. Nowhere is the mingling of divine sovereignty and human responsibility better seen than at the cross, where "Jesus, delivered up according to the definite plan and foreknowledge of God, [was] crucified and killed by the hands of lawless men" (Acts 2:23; see also 4:27–28).

Personal Implications

Take time to reflect on the implications of Joshua 9:1–12:24 for your life. How does this passage lead you to praise God, repent of sin, and trust in his gracious promises? Write down your reflections under the three headings we have considered and on the passage as a whole.

1. Gospel Glimpses

2. Whole-Bible Connections

3. Theological Soundings

4. Joshua 9:1–12:24

As You Finish This Unit . . .

Reflect in prayer on the stunning stubbornness of human sin, and on the specific ways in the past in which your own rebellion from God took on the kind of irrational insanity of the kings listed in these chapters. Praise God for his mighty power to conquer his enemies and keep his promises.

Definitions

[1] **Guilt** – Responsibility for wrongdoing.

[2] **Miracle** – A special act of God that goes beyond natural means, thus demonstrating God's power.

Week 8: Putting Down Roots, Receiving God's Inheritance

Joshua 13:1–19:51

Chapter 13 begins a new chapter in Israel's life under Joshua's leadership. This transition can be seen in the appearance of a new word in the story: inheritance. It appeared just once in the first half of the book (Josh. 11:23), but will occur 56 times from chapter 13 on. Though some areas of Canaan remain unconquered, the conquest is over and Israel is ready to settle the land. These chapters record the meticulous, specific, and at times seemingly monotonous division of the land. Nevertheless, there are a number of important insights to gain from these detailed land assignments.

The Big Picture

Through Joshua the Lord divides the land among his people in such a way as to communicate his divine leadership in the process.

► Reflection and Discussion

Read through Joshua 13:1–19:51, then engage with this section of Scripture using the questions below. (For further background, see the *ESV Study Bible*, pages 415–424; available online at esv.org.)

Tucked into this catalog of land deeds are a number of valuable insights. To start, list themes in this section that are familiar from the story of Joshua to this point. Then, list themes that are new to this section of the book.

One ominous reality hinted at previously is repeated now in such a way that it cannot be missed (see Josh. 13:13; 15:63; 16:10; 17:12–13). This series of qualifications to an otherwise positive distribution of land indicates a problem in the heart of Israel. What is this refrain, and what was the problem at heart?

Another refrain in this section concerns the tribe of Levi. Five times we read, "To the tribe of Levi alone Moses gave no inheritance." Levi did have an inheritance, but of a different kind. Read 13:14; 13:33; and 18:7. What was this special arrangement intended to teach Israel about her physical inheritance?

The Levites weren't given land, but rather "cities to dwell in" among the people (14:4). Given the Levites' priestly functions (see Lev. 10:11; Deut. 33:8–11), including instruction in the Law, what might we suppose was God's intention in spreading them around?

After the eastern allotments were complete (Josh. 13:1–33), the western allotments began. But first attention must be given to a special case: Caleb. Caleb was one of the original 12 spies, standing alone with Joshua 40 years earlier with confidence in God's provision of the land. He remains confident in God's promises and unwavering in the face of the remaining Canaanite inhabitants (14:12). Three times in this section it is said of Caleb, he "wholly followed the LORD" (14:8, 9, 14). How does Caleb's life teach us to follow the Lord wholly? For help, use the contrast between Caleb and the other spies recorded in Numbers 13:30–31 and 14:21–24.

Judah is first in the distribution and receives a disproportionate amount of land. Why might this be? See Genesis 49:8–12 for a hint.

In Joshua 19:51 we learn where these allotments took place: "at Shiloh before the LORD, at the entrance of the tent of meeting." Combined with the method of casting lots, what do these features of the allotment teach Israel about her life in the land?

Read through the following *Gospel Glimpses*, *Whole-Bible Connections*, and *Theological Soundings*. Then take time to consider the *Personal Implications* these reflections have for your walk with the Lord.

Gospel Glimpses

YAHWEH IS OUR INHERITANCE. At one level, the inheritance given to Israel is land, but at another it is the Lord himself. By distributing the land by lot outside the tent of meeting, the Lord conveyed his benevolent presence and rule among them (Josh. 19:51). The Lord's presence is what is good about the land, and this is reinforced by the refrain concerning the Levites: "The LORD God of Israel is their inheritance" (13:33). This is the background to Paul's statement in the New Testament that the Spirit is the "guarantee of our inheritance" (Eph. 1:14). Unlike land, our inheritance as Christians is "imperishable, undefiled, and unfading" (1 Pet. 1:4), for Christ brings a new covenant of unending and uninhibited access to God (Heb. 9:15).

FROM WRATH TO WHOLEHEARTED FOLLOWER OF THE LORD. This is the first time Caleb is mentioned in the book, but he's no latecomer to Israel's story. Caleb and Joshua have grown old together and now they bookend the land's distribution. Caleb is mentioned first because Moses promised him a specific place and because he "wholly followed the LORD" (Josh. 14:8, 9, 14). Caleb's faithfulness is compelling: he treasured the Lord's Word, persevered under trial, and maintained courageous and energetic obedience into old age. Interestingly, though, Caleb's story goes back further than we might think, for Caleb is a Kenizzite (14:6), one of the tribes mentioned in a string of peoples inhabiting the land when God promised it to Abraham (Gen. 15:18–21). In other words, this wholehearted follower of the Lord who is to receive an inheritance comes from a people originally marked for God's wrath. In like manner the Lord's purpose to bless the nations comes to us, former enemies who receive a blessed inheritance through faith in Christ.

Whole-Bible Connections

TENSION IN THE STORYLINE. In the course of dividing the land, an ominous qualification is offered: "Yet the people of Israel did not drive out the Geshurites or the Maacathites, but Geshur and Maacath dwell in the midst of Israel to this day" (Josh. 13:13; see also 15:63; 16:10; 17:12–13). The story of Joshua is mostly optimistic. But this growing refrain portends a haunting reality: the victory has been sweeping, but what remains could spoil it all (Lev. 18:24–25; 20:1–5). Israel's failure of faith is clear from their trepidation before "all the Canaanites who dwell in the plain [that] have chariots of iron" (17:16). These refrains create tension in the storyline of Joshua, which leads us to Christ, the only answer to human sin.

EPHRAIM, JUDAH, AND GOD'S CHOICE. At the start of chapter 16 you may notice a peculiarity. Joshua 16:4 reads, "The people of Joseph, Manasseh and Ephraim, received their inheritance." Yet in verse 5, Ephraim receives an inheritance first, opposite his birth order. This subtle swapping of order highlights God's sovereign designs in the story of salvation. In Genesis 48, against human convention (and their father Joseph's expectation), Jacob blessed Ephraim with priority over Manasseh (Gen. 48:1–22). Likewise, a generation earlier, Jacob was chosen over Esau, and Isaac over Ishmael the generation before that; so goes much of the story of the Bible. Judah was not the oldest or particularly virtuous, but God chose Judah so that Israel's future ruler would come from his loins (Gen. 49:8–12). So it is witnessed again: salvation—in its planning and accomplishment—is entirely of the Lord.

Theological Soundings

FORETASTE OF THE FUTURE. Every Israelite who made their home in Canaan would eventually die there. Thankfully, however, the land functions as a foretaste of the new creation, the consummation[1] of God's plan. Abraham understood this and "desire[d] a better country, that is, a heavenly one" (Heb. 11:16), and Paul, recognizing the global scope of the promise, spoke of Abraham's offspring as "heir of the world" (Rom. 4:13). Abraham's hope is symbolically described in Revelation 21, where John describes his vision of "a new heaven and a new earth," a place where "the dwelling place of God is with man," and where "he will wipe away every tear from their eyes, and death shall be no more" (Rev. 21:1, 3–4). Connecting Joshua's story with this hope, Ezekiel describes this future age with the symbolism of "land" and "inheritance" (Ezek. 47:13–14; compare Josh. 1:6). While Ezekiel and Revelation describe this final state with symbolism, this new creation will be no less physical than Israel's boundaries and towns across Canaan (1 Corinthians 15).

LEVITES AND ISRAEL'S ACCESS TO GOD. Leviticus provides background for the book of Joshua. God set apart the Levites to instruct God's people in his Word and to offer sacrifices for sin on their behalf. This is how Israel may live with God in her midst and yet not die. On the Day of Atonement[2] (Leviticus 16), the Lord required Israel to approach him through an acceptable priest (Lev. 16:1–11), in an acceptable place (Lev. 16:16–19), with an acceptable sacrifice (vv. 20–22). This is how Israel related to God in the land, but this system could not finally deal with the problem it addressed. Instead, the Levitical priesthood, with its tabernacle and sacrificial system, was preparation for Christ, who would sinlessly enter God's true temple and offer the final sacrifice for sin (Hebrews 7–10). This helps us understand the meaning of the work of Christ.

> ## Personal Implications

Take time to reflect on the implications of Joshua 13:1–19:51 for your life. How does this passage lead you to praise God, repent of sin, and trust in his gracious promises? Write down your reflections under the three headings we have considered and on the passage as a whole.

1. Gospel Glimpses

2. Whole-Bible Connections

3. Theological Soundings

4. Joshua 13:1–19:51

▶ As You Finish This Unit . . .

Praise God for the inheritance that is ours in Christ through faith, an eternal and heavenly inheritance that is better than any land. Pray for this hope to strengthen you for wholehearted loyalty to the Lord.

Definitions

[1] **Consummation** – In Christian theology, the final and full establishment of the kingdom of God, when the heavens and earth will be made new and God will rule over all things forever (2 Pet. 3:13; Revelation 11; 19–22).

[2] **Day of Atonement** – The holiest day in the Israelite calendar, when atonement was made for all the sins of Israel from the past year (Leviticus 16). It occurred on the tenth day of the seventh month (September/October), and all Israel was to fast and do no work. Only on that day each year could someone—the high priest—enter the Most Holy Place of the tabernacle (later, the temple) and offer the necessary sacrifices. Also, a "scapegoat" would be sent into the wilderness as a sign of Israel's sins being carried away.

WEEK 9:
CITIES FOR JUSTICE,
PEOPLE FOR WORSHIP

Joshua 20:1–21:45

The Place of the Passage

Joshua 20–21 gives us a closer look at life in the land for Israel in two areas—criminal justice and worship—based on what Moses had said they should do when they entered the land. At first glance, as with other parts of Joshua, it may appear there isn't much here for the New Testament Christian. But with some reflection, there is much to learn. This section closes with a God-exalting summary of all that has happened to this point in the narrative.

The Big Picture

Joshua carries out Moses' instructions for Israel's life under the Lord in the areas of criminal justice and worship.

Reflection and Discussion

Read through Joshua 20:1–21:45, then reflect on this section of Scripture using the questions below. (For further background, see the *ESV Study Bible*, pages 424–426; available online at esv.org.)

1. Cities of Refuge (20:1–9)

This chapter opens with a command from the Lord to appoint cities of refuge according to Moses' instruction. Read the background to this in Numbers 35:9–34. What factors distinguish murder from manslaughter?

As you read the Joshua and Numbers passages, who are the parties involved in determining a killer's fate?

What does this arrangement teach us about God? What does this passage teach us about mankind?

Israel's theocracy was unique to this stage in God's salvation plan. Given that these laws assumed certain realities about God, human dignity, and human sin, do we find any principles we can apply to the administration of justice elsewhere?

What might be the significance of the manslayer's waiting to leave his place of refuge until the death of the high priest? Numbers 35:26–28 provides a clue.

2. Cities for Levites (21:1–45)

Why don't the Levites get an inheritance like the rest of Israel's tribes?

Joshua 21:41 tells us the Levites were spread throughout the nation. Given their function in Israel's life, what was God's purpose in this placement of the Levites?

With the land now divided, the last three verses of this chapter summarize all that the Lord has done for his people. What three things has the Lord given to Israel? What key verb is repeated?

God's sovereignty in Israel's salvation is plain. What response should this evoke from us as we reflect on our own salvation?

Read through the following *Gospel Glimpses, Whole-Bible Connections,* and *Theological Soundings.* Then take time to consider the *Personal Implications* these reflections have for your walk with the Lord.

Gospel Glimpses

WORTH OF HUMAN LIFE. A certain view of human beings undergirds all of Joshua 20. According to Genesis 1:27, "God created man in his own image." Human beings are like God in important ways, representing him in the world. An affront to any human being is an affront to God. This is why death is given as a penalty for murder (Gen. 9:6; see also James 3:9). The inestimable worth of humanity could not be clearer than on the cross of Christ. There Jesus, having become fully human, died a human death for the redemption of human beings (Heb. 2:14).

THE LORD GIVES WHAT HE PROMISES. As we have learned, the Bible is a story of promise and fulfillment held together by a series of unfolding covenants. The book of Joshua is one installment in this story. While the story of the Old Testament recounts dark days for Israel, the story of Joshua is largely encouraging. The people have generally obeyed, and the Lord has given them land through many powerful victories—just as he promised. This is why this section ends by referring to the "good promises that the LORD had made . . . [which] came to pass" (Josh. 21:45). Likewise today we glorify God for all he has brought to pass in Christ. As Paul says, "All the promises of God find their Yes in him" (2 Cor. 1:20).

Whole-Bible Connections

A STORY OF SUBSTITUTION. If the manslayer leaves the city of refuge and is killed by the avenger, the avenger is not guilty (Num. 35:26–28). However, if he leaves after the high priest's death, the avenger may not kill him. We may presume that the high priest's death serves as a substitute for the manslayer's death. This is consistent with the pattern of substitution in Scripture. While the emphasis of Joshua is on the land, sacrifice and substitution are also vital to the story. The celebration of the Passover and the presence of the Levites reinforce sin's penalty and God's provision. Later the prophet Isaiah would speak of the One to come who would be "crushed for our iniquities" (Isa. 53:5). All of this looks forward to Jesus Christ, our Great High Priest, who accomplished a substitutionary atonement when he "put away sin" once and for all "by the sacrifice of himself" (Heb. 9:26).

LEVITES AMONG GOD'S PEOPLE. When we see the priests spread around the land, this should call to mind their specific function in the life of Israel: to instruct the people in the Word and to represent the people to God through the tabernacle[1] and the sacrificial system. Every sacrifice offered for sin was a reminder of sin, its penalty, and the inadequacy of animal sacrifices to make atonement (Heb. 10:3–4).

Theological Soundings

GOD, HUMANS, AND HUMAN GOVERNMENT. The Sinaitic covenant is not a pattern for government in general. Still, suppositions in Israel's life about God, the world, and human nature have a bearing on our own practices in government. The protections and consequences for taking life assume human dignity. Murder and vengeance assume human sinfulness. The requirement of two witnesses, with agreement from the congregation, assumes finite human knowledge and perception, and also the imperfect nature of human justice. Universal access to safety, checks on human power, the presumption of innocence, considerations for intent and motive, and punishments that fit crimes (Ex. 21:23–25) are all elements worthy of consideration for government wherever it is found.

COHERENCE OF GOD'S INERRANT[2] WORD. Joshua 21:45 is a sweeping description of how well things have gone for Israel: "Not one word of all the good promises that the LORD had made to the house of Israel had failed." But since Canaanite land and inhabitants remain unconquered, is this statement true (see 23:1–5)? Some say Joshua is really a patchwork of material stitched together without a divine author behind it, but an understanding of literary genre can help us grasp the coherence of God's Word: Joshua is a work of prophetic history. That is, this is history with a theological purpose. If we assume one author, we may assume this writer meant us to interpret any given part of the book in light of the whole: of course there is unfinished business, but the point of emphasis is the Lord's faithfulness to his promises.

Personal Implications

Take time to reflect on the implications of Joshua 20:1–21:45 for your life. How does this passage lead you to praise God, repent of sin, and trust in his gracious promises? Write down your reflections under the three headings we have considered and on the passage as a whole.

1. Gospel Glimpses

2. Whole-Bible Connections

3. Theological Soundings

4. Joshua 20:1–21:45

As You Finish This Unit . . .

Praise God for his creation of humankind in his image and for his justice and protection through human government. Thank him for all of the good promises he has given and fulfilled for us in Christ.

Definitions

[1] **Tabernacle** – The tent where God dwelled on earth and communed with his people Israel as their divine king. Also referred to as the "tent of meeting" (Lev. 1:5). The temple in Jerusalem later replaced it.

[2] **Inerrancy** – The doctrine of biblical inerrancy expresses the Bible's own teaching that it is true, reliable, and trustworthy—without error—in all the matters that it affirms and addresses (2 Tim. 3:16).

Week 10: An Altar of Remembrance, an Unforgettable Altercation

Joshua 22:1–34

▲

Joshua 22 is the beginning of the end. The conquest is over and the land has been divided among the tribes. Chapters 22, 23, and 24 each begin with a parting speech from Joshua. He speaks to the eastern tribes, to Israel's leadership, and finally to all of Israel. Here in chapter 22, Joshua speaks to the tribes who came over the Jordan with the rest of Israel but whose inheritance had already been won east of the Jordan. The time has come for them to return home. When they do, the story takes an unexpected turn to one of the most intense moments in the book. The outcome is equally as unexpected and makes for a stronger and more unified nation.

After Joshua sends Israel's eastern tribes home with a parting speech, a surprising turn of events leads to a more cohesive nation.

> ## Reflection and Discussion

Read Joshua 22:1–34, then interact with this section of Scripture using the questions below. (For further background, see the *ESV Study Bible*, pages 426–428; available online at esv.org.)

1. Joshua's Parting Speech to the Eastern Tribes (22:1–6)

In Joshua's words to the eastern tribes are a commendation for careful obedience (22:2–3) and a command for faithfulness to Moses' law (v. 5). We may be tempted to think of commands as rigid and unhappy things, but here in verses 5–6 we get a positive, relational picture of obedience. Paying attention to verbs, write a list of what God requires of his people.

Read Deuteronomy 6:1–3 for background to Joshua's exhortation. What rewards did Moses promise for this kind of obedience?

According to Deuteronomy 6:4–9, what else were the Israelites supposed to do with God's commands?

2. A Suspicious Altar and a Declaration of War (22:7–20)

This section develops a conflict revolving around an "altar of imposing size" (Josh. 22:10). Three passages will provide the needed context. Read Deuteronomy 6:10–19; 12:1–14; and Numbers 25:1–9 for background. What was the perceived problem with this altar? To help focus your answer, look ahead to Joshua 22:29.

What does the response of the western tribes indicate about their spiritual condition?

In what way did the western tribes demonstrate wisdom in this confrontation? In what way did they demonstrate grace?

3. A Unifying Exchange and Proof of the Lord's Presence (22:21–34)

In verses 21–23 the eastern tribes express an important point of agreement. What is it?

Read Deuteronomy 6:10–25 for background into the intentions of the eastern tribes. No doubt they remembered the reading of the law at the altar on Mount Ebal (Josh. 8:30–35). It was a commitment to this law of Moses that led them to build this copy of the altar as a witness to their unity as a nation. Thus this imposing altar was actually a sign of the same spiritual sobriety shared by the tribes west of the Jordan. A very bad ending is averted and replaced with an extraordinary ending. List here each indication of a positive outcome.

Why do you suppose the Lord allowed this conflict in Israel's life? What is an implication of the exclusivity of God's tabernacle (22:29) for Christians today?

Read Hebrews 9:1–14 and compare the two tents contrasted there. Then, reflecting on the exclusivity of Christ and his cross for salvation, rewrite Joshua 22:29 as your own commitment to the Lord.

Read through the following *Gospel Glimpses, Whole-Bible Connections,* and *Theological Soundings.* Then take time to consider the *Personal Implications* these reflections have for your walk with the Lord.

Gospel Glimpses

CLING TO THE LORD. The description of what it means to obey Moses' law is remarkable, especially Joshua's command to "cling to him" (Josh. 22:5; see also 23:8). This corrects any notion that God's commands are dry or impersonal and gets to the heart of what God really wants from us. Such obedience is incompatible with clinging to this world, so the Lord will warn Israel about clinging to other gods in the next chapter (23:12). In Jesus Christ we see the embodiment of what it means to cling to the Lord, and through Jesus we are compelled to cling to Yahweh for life. Like a child clings to his father for protection, provision, and love, so we cling to our Lord for the same.

ONE PEOPLE FOR GOD. Nothing more tragic could be imagined for the eastern tribes than for their children to be separated from Israel west of the river. As God is one, so are his people. So it is for God's new covenant people, the church, in an even deeper way. Not all in Israel truly belonged to God, because not all believed as Abraham did (Rom. 2:28–29). In the new covenant community, however, everyone knows the Lord (Jer. 31:34). This new people is Christ's new humanity, the eschatological fulfillment of God's promise that Abraham's offspring would bless the nations (Gen. 22:18; Gal. 3:8; Eph. 2:11–21).

Whole-Bible Connections

THE LAW OF MOSES AND THE LAW OF CHRIST. For Israel, keeping the Book of Moses was a matter of life and death, blessing and curse. Is it for us? Yes and no. God does require the fulfillment of all his commands. But because of Jesus' obedience and curse-bearing sacrifice (Gal. 3:10–14), the law is no longer a barrier between God and us. Through his new covenant work, Jesus fulfilled the law so that it is now obsolete (Matt. 5:17; Heb. 8:13). But this doesn't mean that the law is not instructive for us, for many of its commands are tied to the nature of God, human beings, and creation. Murder and adultery, for example, are still wrong. But since Christians today live by the "law of Christ," such things as anger and lust are also wrong, since they violate the law of love that unites all of God's commands (Rom. 13:9–10; 1 Cor. 9:21; Gal. 6:2). Indeed, the life of a Christian is loftier than anything required by Moses' law, but so is the power that believers receive from the Holy Spirit.

REAL POSSIBILITY OF APOSTASY.[1] It is possible for someone to say he belongs to God and be lying or self-deceived. That is what appears to be the case in Joshua 22. The western tribes' response confronts the seriousness of abandoning the Lord. Wisely, they listened to the eastern tribes before executing them. New Testament Christians don't swing swords, but that doesn't mean apostasy is less serious. It is actually more serious. To those who call Jesus "Lord" but are deceived, Jesus will say, "I never knew you; depart from me" (Matt. 7:21–23). Of two who abandoned the faith, Paul said, "I have handed [them] over to Satan" (1 Tim. 1:20). This responsibility belongs to the entire new covenant community. After a patient and increasingly public restorative process of pleading, without repentance,[2] Jesus says, "Let [the unrepentant person] be to you as a Gentile" (Matt. 18:17). This verdict is more severe than any physical judgment, for as Jesus warns, "Do not fear those who kill the body but cannot kill the soul. Rather fear him who can destroy both soul and body in hell" (Matt. 10:28).

Theological Soundings

FUTURE-ORIENTED FAITH. The eastern tribes were looking to the future when they built their own copy of the altar. This future orientation is natural to every believer in every place in God's salvation story. After the fall into sin, Adam named his wife Eve, which means "mother of all living" (Gen. 3:20). Abraham, Moses, Joshua, David, and the rest of the Old Testament faithful "died in faith, not having received the things promised, but having seen them and greeted them from afar" (Heb. 11:13). So today, as Peter says, "According to his promise we are waiting for new heavens and a new earth in which righteousness dwells" (2 Pet. 3:13). This helps us understand that faith is not just mental assent but a forward-looking anticipation.

ONE ALTAR FOR ONE WAY TO GOD. God requires us to come to him on his terms. The eastern and western tribes both recognized this in the exclusivity of the tabernacle for approaching God. Just as the tabernacle was Israel's one way of relating to God, now Christ has made complete access to God possible through the one altar at Calvary. This is what the book of Hebrews tells us. Israel's tabernacle provided imperfect access to God through imperfect sacrifices and an imperfect priesthood. Jesus enters once with his own blood and secures for us an eternal redemption (Heb. 9:1–14). Jesus is the only way to God because his cross is the only possible way for sinners to stand before God and not die.

Personal Implications

Take time to reflect on the implications of Joshua 22:1–34 for your life. How does this passage lead you to praise God, repent of sin, and trust in his gracious promises? Write down your reflections under the three headings we have considered and on the passage as a whole.

1. Gospel Glimpses

2. Whole-Bible Connections

3. Theological Soundings

4. Joshua 22:1–34

> **As You Finish This Unit . . .**

Pray for the unity of God's one people around God's one altar for salvation, Calvary. Pray as well for a sobriety about sin born of a conviction that God's Word is true, we are great sinners, and there is only one way to be right with him.

Definitions

[1] **Apostasy** – Abandonment or renunciation of faith.

[2] **Repentance** – A complete change of heart and mind regarding one's overall attitude toward God or one's individual actions. True regeneration and conversion are always accompanied by repentance.

Week 11: Joshua Dies in the Land, the Promise of Rest Lives On

Joshua 23:1–24:33

The Place of the Passage

Chapters 23 and 24 both begin with a parting speech from Joshua, who is now "old and well advanced in years" (23:1). The first speech is to Israel's leaders, and the second to the nation. While Joshua's speeches are optimistic in many ways, they also indicate much unfinished business and uncertainty concerning Israel's future. Joshua is excited for all that God has done, yet frustrated by the superficiality of the people's allegiance. This tension between God's promises and Israel's disobedience is a theme throughout the Old Testament. It is a problem for which the coming of Christ (and the new covenant) provides the only solution. As Joshua breathes his last, this chapter cries out for the greater Joshua to come.

The Big Picture

Joshua issues parting speeches to Israel's leaders and the nation, each speech rehearsing God's glorious promises and charting the way forward for the nation.

> **Reflection and Discussion**

Read through Joshua 23:1–24:33, then study this section of Scripture utilizing the questions below. (For further background, see the *ESV Study Bible*, pages 428–431; available online at esv.org.)

1. Joshua's Parting Speech to Israel's Leaders (23:1–16)

The book of Joshua opened with God's commission of Joshua, a charge filled with promises and commands. Now Joshua says to his leaders, "You have seen all that the LORD your God has done" (23:3). Paying attention to the verbs in Joshua's speech, list what the Lord has done and will do.

As we've come to expect, mingled among these promises is a number of commands. List what Joshua commands the people to do.

What is at stake in Israel's obedience or disobedience? Recall our study to this point—what is the covenantal context for this pattern?

If God makes promises contingent on obedience, how do you suppose those promises will ever be fulfilled, given human sinfulness?

2. Joshua's Parting Speech to the Nation (24:1–28)

Joshua's final speech begins with a rehearsal of Israel's history in 24:2–13. Again, paying attention to the verbs, list all that Joshua records concerning God's work on Israel's behalf.

Paying special notice to verses 12–13, note what point the Lord is making in this speech to Israel. What should Israel be feeling at the conclusion of this brief review of her history?

In verses 14–15, Joshua commands the people to "fear the LORD and serve him in sincerity and in faithfulness" and to "Put away" their false gods, choosing whom they will serve. Why doesn't Joshua give these commands at the beginning of his speech?

Time and again Israel is warned against serving other gods. Using descriptions of God and his ways in this chapter, finish the following sentence in at least five ways: "When Israel serves other gods, she . . ." (for example: denies, forgets, clings, etc.).

The exchange between Joshua and Israel in verses 14–28 is a bit of a surprise. Read Deuteronomy 31:21–29. What did Moses and Joshua know about Israel that God's people struggled to understand?

3. Joshua's Death (24:29–33)

The book of Joshua begins with the death of Moses and ends with the death of Joshua. With the death of every person, especially every leader, comes an important reminder for God's people. What is that reminder?

As the story of Joshua comes to a conclusion, we can be grateful that the story of the Bible is not over. Read Hebrews 3–4 and 11:1–12:2. List all the commands given to New Testament Christians on the basis of the Old Testament story.

Read through the following *Gospel Glimpses, Whole-Bible Connections,* and *Theological Soundings.* Then take time to consider the *Personal Implications* these reflections have for your walk with the Lord.

Gospel Glimpses

THE LORD GIVES REST. Through Joshua, the Lord gave rest to his people in the land. But this rest is neither secure nor complete. Enemy nations remained in the land because sin remained in Israel. Many years later King David would say to his people, "Today, if you hear his voice, do not harden your hearts," reminding them of what God said concerning Moses' generation: "They shall not enter my rest" (Ps. 95:7–11). Reflecting on this, the author of Hebrews draws an important conclusion: "If Joshua had given them rest, God would not have spoken of another day later on. So then, there remains a Sabbath rest for the people of God" (Heb. 4:8–9). Joshua did not bring true rest, but Jesus does. Christians have entered God's rest by means of abiding faith in the perfect obedience and sacrifice of our Great High Priest, Jesus Christ (Heb. 3:7–4:16), and we strive daily for the full realization and enjoyment of this salvation (4:3, 11).

THE LORD GIVES VICTORY. In Joshua's final speech he sets the conquest of the land in the broader story of the nation, a story of the Lord's making. God called Abraham, he sent plagues on Egypt, and he parted waters at the Red Sea. So, too, the conquest was his work. Twice the Lord says, "I gave them into your hand" (Josh. 24:8, 11). The message is plain: "It was not by your sword or by your bow. I gave you a land on which you had not labored and cities that you had not built, and you dwell in them" (vv. 12–13). In Christ, God defeats Satan and death, the enemies that stand behind all others. But he does so not by the sword, for at his arrest Jesus told Peter to put his sword away (John 18:11). Rather, he does so by means of his cross (Heb. 2:14–17). On the cross Jesus suffered the wrath both of God's enemies and of God himself as a sacrifice for sin.

THE LORD GIVES LAND. The theme of land is the stage and subject for all the action in Joshua. Its possession was an installation in God's fulfillment of his promise to Abraham (Josh. 23:14). For Israel it represented the place where everything would be right, their oppressors would be gone, and the presence of the Lord would be known. That sounds wonderful, yet Hebrews says that this and everything tied to Moses is but a "shadow" of our ultimate hope (Heb. 8:5; 10:1). Even Abraham expected more than mere Canaan, considering his people "strangers and exiles on the earth." Instead, with him we seek a new creation, a city "whose designer and builder is God" (Heb. 11:8–16).

87

Whole-Bible Connections

PROMISE AND FULFILLMENT, BLESSING AND CURSE. Joshua's final speeches are rich with fulfillment: "Not one word has failed of all the good things that the LORD your God promised concerning you" (Josh. 21:45). Yet some of God's promises are not so good, as Joshua indicates that Israel's story will get worse before it gets better. Exile[1] is threatened (23:13–16) as a consequence of disobedience, and 24:19 essentially seals their fate: "You are not able to serve the LORD." This echoes Moses' words in Deuteronomy 31:29, where he predicted that the people would not actually obey, would go into exile, and would need God to regather them and give them new hearts (Deut. 30:1–6). They can commit to serve God all they want (Josh. 24:23–24), but Joshua agrees with Moses: their hearts will lead them astray (see Deut. 31:21, 27). How can God's promises be realized when Israel's obedience is only partial at best? The Sinaitic covenant is no solution. What is needed is a new covenant, as the prophets anticipate. Jeremiah 31 speaks of the full forgiveness of sins, the law written on the heart, and perfect communion with God (see also Ezek. 36:22–32). Through his broken body and shed blood, Jesus brings this new covenant (Luke 22:19–20). Through Christ, God removes his wrath from us, for "Christ redeemed us from the curse of the law by becoming a curse for us" (Gal. 3:13), and through Christ the Lord has blessed us "with every spiritual blessing in the heavenly places" (Eph. 1:3).

JOSHUA, SERVANT OF THE LORD. The book began by calling Moses the Lord's servant. Fifteen times Moses has been called God's servant (Josh. 1:1, 7, 13, 15; 8:31; etc.). Now, for the first time, Joshua is given the same title (24:29). Still, the author of Hebrews will contrast this honorable position with Jesus' greater position as more than a servant: a son over God's house (Heb. 3:5–6).

Theological Soundings

JOSHUA DIED BUT JESUS WAS RAISED.[2] For all of our ambition and technology, humans have not solved the problem of death. It comes to the rich and the poor alike, to the just and the unjust (Eccles. 9:2), and even giants of the faith like Joshua "go the way of all the earth" (Josh. 23:14). Even Joseph's bones, carried back into the land (24:32), remind us that the greatest men die. Thankfully, while there is no merely human answer to death, there is a divine answer in the resurrection of Jesus Christ. Without this the Christian faith is futile (1 Cor. 15:17–19). However, because Jesus has been raised from the dead, we too "will be raised imperishable, and we shall be changed" (1 Cor. 15:52). This is why we don't grieve as those who have no hope (1 Thess. 4:13) but can say with the apostle Paul, "'O death, where is your victory? O death, where is your sting?' . . . Thanks be to God, who gives us the victory through our Lord Jesus Christ" (1 Cor. 15:54–57).

CHOOSE THIS DAY. There is urgency in Joshua's voice as he speaks to his people for the last time: "Choose this day whom you will serve" (Josh. 24:15). In his old age Joshua feels the shortness of life and the urgency of serving the Lord. David felt that same urgency when he wrote, "Today, if you hear his voice, do not harden your hearts" (Ps. 95:7), and the author of Hebrews, quoting David, calls the church to exercise the same kind of daily urgency together: "Take care, brothers, lest there be in any of you an evil, unbelieving heart, leading you to fall away from the living God. But exhort one another every day, as long as it is called 'today,' that none of you may be hardened by the deceitfulness of sin" (Heb. 3:12–13). Repentance and faith are necessary for salvation, and *now* is always the time to respond to God (see 2 Cor. 6:2).

Personal Implications

Take time to reflect on the implications of Joshua 23:1–24:33 for your life. How does this passage lead you to praise God, repent of sin, and trust in his gracious promises? Write down your reflections under the three headings we have considered and on the passage as a whole.

1. Gospel Glimpses

2. Whole-Bible Connections

3. Theological Soundings

----

4. Joshua 23:1–24:33

As You Finish This Unit . . .

Confess to God that you have not loved him or clung to him as you should; praise God for his provision of a greater Joshua and obedient Savior in Christ; and resolve to serve the Lord with your life as you rest in him and wait for your eternal and heavenly inheritance.

Definitions

[1] **The exile** – Several relocations of large groups of Israelites/Jews have occurred throughout history, but "the exile" typically refers to the Babylonian exile, that is, Nebuchadnezzar's relocation of residents of the southern kingdom of Judah to Babylon in 586 BC. (Residents of the northern kingdom of Israel had been resettled by Assyria in 722 BC.) After Babylon came under Persian rule, several waves of Jewish exiles returned and repopulated Judah.

[2] **Resurrection** – The impartation of new, eternal life to a dead person at the end of time (or in the case of Jesus, on the third day after his death). This new life is not a mere resuscitation of the body (as in the case of Lazarus; John 11:1–44) but a transformation of the body to an eternal state (1 Cor. 15:35–58). Both the righteous and the wicked will be resurrected, the former to eternal life and the latter to judgment (John 5:29).

Week 12: Summary and Conclusion

▲

We will conclude our study of Joshua by summarizing the big picture of God's message through Joshua as a whole. Then we will consider several questions in order to reflect on various *Gospel Glimpses*, *Whole-Bible Connections*, and *Theological Soundings* throughout the entire book.

The Big Picture of Joshua

Between the death of Moses and the death of Joshua, Israel moved into the land. Joshua tells this story. This is clear from the very structure of the book: after making preparations and crossing into the land (Joshua 1–5), Joshua and Israel took the land (chs. 6–12), divided the land (chs. 13–21), and committed themselves to the Lord's service in the land (chs. 22–24).

However, while Joshua is a story about land, land is more than geography, for this is the land of promise—God's promise. Joshua is a story about the God who makes and keeps his promises, about the problem of sin that landed humanity outside of Eden, and about the just judgment sin deserves. In light of the fullness of God's revelation, Joshua is also a story about the kind of Savior Christ is, the kind of people Christ saves, and the kind of salvation Christ brings. Joshua takes Israel into the land with the ark. Jesus takes us into

God's presence through a cross. Appropriately, Joshua's name is the Hebrew form of Jesus, meaning "Yahweh Saves."

Today, Christians enjoy the certain hope of a place more wonderful than Israel's land of promise: a new creation (Revelation 21–22). Even the best years in the land of promise would be characterized by sin and death. But in the New Jerusalem—another way to speak of the new creation—death and sin and pain will be no more. There, God's people will be perfected to rest in enjoyment of God's presence for all eternity. And all of this because Jesus, the new and better Joshua, came to "save his people from their sins" through perfect obedience to God's perfect Word (Matt. 1:21; Josh. 1:9).

Gospel Glimpses

The book of Joshua is rich with insight into God's gracious plan to save sinners. He saves through an obedient leader (Josh. 1:8); he saves those who demonstrate faith in God and his promises, including many Gentiles marked out for wrath; and his salvation leads into the enjoyment of his presence, as his people cling to him for rest. Joshua brings these things in part, but Jesus brings them in whole by taking on himself the judgment his people deserve. This is what rest in God's presence will ultimately require. This is the gospel.

How has Joshua brought new clarity to your understanding of the gospel?

What particular passages or themes in Joshua have led you to a fresh understanding and grasp of God's grace to us through Jesus?

In our journey into the land with Joshua, we've seen many turns in the story: the Lord gave Israel the land, gave her victory in battle, and extended salvation to Gentiles. This is a story of great expectation and fulfillment. And yet along the way we've picked up reminders of the presence and persistence of sin. The Sinaitic Covenant, with its blessings and curses, Levitical priesthood, and tabernacle and ark, wasn't able to return humanity to Eden. The human heart remains sick. Thankfully, the book of Joshua is just one turn in the story of the whole Bible. In Christ's new covenant, the themes of land, rest, deliverance, and inheritance take on new dimensions.

How has this study of Joshua amplified your understanding of the biblical storyline of redemption?

What themes emphasized in Joshua helped you deepen your grasp of the Bible's unity?

What passages or themes expanded your understanding of the redemption Jesus provides, begun at his first coming and to be consummated at his return?

What connections between Joshua and the New Testament were new to you?

Theological Soundings

Joshua has much to contribute to Christian theology. Numerous doctrines and themes are developed, clarified, and reinforced throughout Joshua, such as the justice and mercy of God, the active obedience of Christ, the exclusivity of Christ, and God's promise of a new creation.

Has your theology shifted in minor or major ways during the course of studying Joshua? How so?

How has your understanding of the nature and character of God been deepened throughout this study?
